Adrian Anthony McFarlane

A Grammar
of Fear and Evil

A Husserlian-Wittgensteinian
Hermeneutic

PETER LANG
New York • Washington, D.C./Baltimore
Bern • Frankfurt am Main • Berlin • Vienna • Paris

Library of Congress Cataloging-in-Publication Data
McFarlane, Adrian Anthony
A grammar of fear and evil: a Husserlian-Wittgensteinian
hermeneutic/ Adrian Anthony McFarlane.
p. cm. — (Studies in European thought; vol. 9)
Includes bibliographical references.
1. Fear. 2. Good and evil. 3. Hermeneutics. 4. Phenomenology. 5. Ordinary-
language philosophy. 6. Husserl, Edmund, 1859–1938. 7. Wittgenstein,
Ludwig, 1889–1951. I. Title. II. Series.
BD440.M34   128'.3—dc20   95-34835
ISBN 0-8204-3046-3
ISSN 1043-5786

Die Deutsche Bibliothek-CIP-Einheitsaufnahme

McFarlane, Adrian Anthony:
A grammar of fear and evil: a Husserlian-Wittgensteinian hermeneutic/ Adrian
Anthony McFarlane. –New York; Washington, D.C./Baltimore; Bern;
Frankfurt am Main; Berlin; Vienna; Paris: Lang.
(Studies in European thought; Vol. 9)
ISBN 0-8204-3046-3
NE: GT

© 1996 Peter Lang Publishing, Inc., New York

Printed in the United States of America.

DEDICATION

In memory of Drs. Winifred D. Wandersee (Dewar Professor of History and Faculty Chair 1991-1994) and Dr. Robert R. Smith (Professor of Biology, Curator of Hoysradt Hebarium, and Director of Pine Lake) of Hartwick College—esteemed colleagues, loyal friends, and exemplary role models—whose scholarship, encouragement, sober sense of justice, and indefatigable courage inspire an **undying** quality of life sufficient to make immortality credible.

Table of Contents

ACKNOWLEDGMENT

The writing, editing and revisions of this manuscript would have proven to be unbearably lonely and fearsome were it not for the support of some very special people.

First, my deep gratitude to **Carol Belles** of Princeton Theological Seminary who challenged, encouraged, and supported me (scribally) in getting started. I thank her and her family. Also, to **Aphro Zulema** and **Regina Azul** who exemplify the undaunting spirit of courage, faith, hope and love—my quintessential paradigms for intentional living.

Second, I am grateful to Professors Robert Corrington, Charles Courtney (Drew University), Dominick Iorio, (Rider University), and James Loder (Princeton Theological Seminary), for having read the manuscript in its early stage and thereafter encouraged me to publish it. Their suggestions and helpful critical comments, along with those of Peter Lang's anonymous reviewers, were most instructive. Along with their support I have been blessed with invaluable secretarial and administrative assistance from Janice Stankiewicz, Melissa Morse and Christina Beebe (who saw the work to its completion). Jan's initial support, Chrissy's editing, secretarial, administrative and logistical skills, and Melissa's keen eyes have greatly allayed my fears of complex details.

Third, I am immeasurably grateful to Dr. Barry Rossman, of Princeton Medical Center, who saw me through my most fearsome experience; and Drs. William Haynes, Gerald Groves, Samuel Swaby, my family, and especially my sister, Nurse Joyce Millicent Johnson, for credible and caring support far beyond ordinary duty and friendship. A special expression of gratitude goes to Professors Connie Anderson and Stanley Konecky (Hartwick College), Reverend Mrs. Nancy Schluter (Chaplain,

x

Rider University), John S. Siffert, Susan L. Sommer, Theresa Burns-Brown, and my son, Dietrich, all of whom walked with me "through the valley of evil and incredible testing"—theirs is a gift of healing and reassuring grace!

I have had the good fortune of praying friends: Eleanor Doty, Elizabeth Frykberg, James Loder, Beryl/Horace Russell, David/Nalini Singh, Gladys Taylor, the Witherspoon Street Presbyterian Church (Princeton), the Tremont Presbyterian Church (Bronx), St. Paul's Kirk (Kingston, Jamaica), First Presbyterian Church (Oneonta), and Christ Church on Quaker Hill (Pawling). All of these persons and assemblies, along with some dear colleagues and students at Hartwick College, have been outstanding in their prayers and encouragement.

Additionally, I am grateful to Hartwick College for granting me a study leave to complete this project. Correspondingly, I am indebted to Dr. John Muddiman and the community at Mansfield College, Oxford University, United Kingdom, for providing a welcoming and resourceful environment in which to think and write during the Michaelmas Term 1994.

Finally, beyond these personal recognitions, grateful acknowledgment is herein expressed for permission, obtained from the publishers/authors, to publish material that was previously printed in the following publications: Marvin Farber: *The Foundation of Phenomenology*, (Albany, NY: SUNY Press) copyright 1962; reprinted with permission of the publisher. Nicholas Gier: *Wittgenstein and Phenomenology*, (Albany, NY: SUNY Press) copyright 1981; reprinted with permission of the publisher. Frederick Ferré: *Language, Logic and God*, (New York, NY: Harper Row Publishers) copyright 1969; reprinted with permission of the author. Herbert Spiegelberg: *Doing*

INTRODUCTION

In this manuscript the phenomenon of fear is examined as a primary context for the problem of evil. It claims that whereas the locution "evil" is primarily a religious interpretation of life's troubling experiences, fear is the primary experience on which this interpretation builds. Thus, the problem of evil has to be seen in the light of the fears which inform our interpretations.

In reducing the problem of evil to the primary context of experience I argue that the challenges of life do not issue from metaphysical sources, but arise in human consciousness. This shifts the focus from causes, divine or otherwise, to the conditions of experience and meaning. In other words, the world only "comes to light" in consciousness.

Against the background of this important tenet of Husserlian phenomenology, the basic structures of **experience** and **interpretation** are examined and analyzed. The range of experience is viewed as: the self, the world, and a possible transphenomenal world; and the range of interpretation as the necessity for identity, power, and enduring significance. I further maintain that the intentional correlation of self and world (in every act of consciousness) is the necessary condition for experience and interpretation, and that the dialectical struggle between identity and difference is the catalyst (and sufficient condition) for interpretation. The one makes experience and meaning possible, while the other extends the borders of the possible. Thus, meaning does not only consist in "givens" articulated by reference, but "discoverables" made known in use.

This latter assessment is the product of Ludwig Wittgenstein's later philosophy which emphasizes the importance of internal relations, as well as the analogical procedures by which relations are made. Both Husserl and Wittgenstein acknowledge that logical grammar holds the "givens" and "discoverables" in creative tension.

A grammar of fear is therefore a description of both the conditions and the modalization of fear. The one deals with the ongoing relations between self and world, while the other deals with the ways in which the relationships are approached. One of the ways of dealing with these relationships is to attribute ultimate significance—evil and goodness—to the threats and securities we experience.

Having given a précis of the content of this work, it might be helpful to the reader to gain some understanding of its background, process, style and method. It is hoped that what follows will function as an aid to dialogue and a catalyst for understanding.

The background of this manuscript is marked by an apparent contrast which, on closer observation, proves to be coincidentally uncanny. To wit, the inspiration for the research began to take shape during the Halloween preparations of 1983; the period in which some were playfully masquerading as ghouls, goblins, vampires, and witches, and when the United States military forces were busy invading the tiny Caribbean island of Grenada. In more ways than those articulated below, this manuscript explores and *shows* the two faces of fear, namely, fear as a destabilizing experience, and as a catalyst for understanding.

To those who are schooled in world affairs, particularly the peculiarities of the East-West ideological "battles," the invasion was, at worst, similar to the former Soviet Union's invasion of Afghanistan. But for me, the Grenada invasion was closer to home and therefore seemed far more threatening. In fact, given the growing regional pride since the late fifties, the invasion is still believed to be the most damaging political act the English speaking Caribbean has experienced this century. It portends the precariousness of political self-determination by small countries, and thereby raises the questions of sovereignty, security, and power.

I began to wrestle with the event by questioning my assumptions about the responsibilities and liabilities of self-determination in small countries. It was then that a colleague reminded me that self-determination is not exercised in a vacuum; rather, it is achieved through struggle. This led me to see that self-determination involves the "coincidence" of power, and that power grows or diminishes in the face of the fears it encounters.

Yet, I continued to ask myself whether defensive action is not the most "civilized" means of combating fear; and if not, how might one justify an offensive act?

These questions were answered for me, though unsatisfactorily, by Edward Seaga, the then Prime Minister of Jamaica, and a staunch United States ally in the invasion. His defense of the invasion was that Grenada was stock-piling weapons far out of proportion to its defense needs, and that its neighbors were fearful of Grenada's (undeclared) aggressive intentions. By implication, there are times when the most adequate means of defense is offensive action—what was euphemistically referred to then as "a pre-emptive strike."

However, as my interest was deeper than the ethics or politics of the invasion (about which I am not competent to advance informed political judgments), I sought to understand instead the conditions for the experience and expression of the fears which this act seems to typify. My preliminary reflections led me to hypothesize that fear is an expression of insecurity, that power is a safeguard for security, and that temporal and transtemporal continuity are the goals of security and power. In short, that the experience of fear makes it evident that any serious quest for the (ultimate) meaning of life requires a constant struggle in our process of becoming.

If only on the surface, it would seem that if fear poses such a serious challenge to experience and meaning, it might also have a relation to the problem of evil. For if meaning *qua* meaning is the most basic form of human consciousness, and consciousness strives to produce and improve (enlarge) the meaning of existence, then the fear of ultimate meaninglessness must be the most critical challenge to the security, power, and enduring significance of life. As such, there seems to be more than a passing relationship between fear and evil.

The main task of this work, therefore, is to investigate this relationship. This I have done by examining the experience of fear and the interpretation which makes the experience intelligible. Thus, Chapter I lays the foundation for the discussion of fear as a complex phenomenon which involves experience and interpretation. This is accomplished by employing the methodology of Husserlian phenomenology.

It will be seen that the phenomenological approach of this study is more than a cataloguing of particular fears, and it is definitely not a psychological study. These approaches are by no means unimportant for this study, but they do not deliver the basic structure which this investigation seeks. That is, a phenomenology of fear is more concerned with the "grammar of fear"—the correlation of the *act* and *object* of consciousness—than with particular fears. Nevertheless, our study does take into account some examples of fear on which the categorial analyses are based.

In this regard, Chapters II and III together constitute an approach to the grammar of fear; the one deals with some basic categories of fear, while the other deals with the problematics of fear.

These tasks are sufficiently compelling to investigate the function of language in experience, and the impact of experience on language. Here the methodology of Husserl's phenomenology is buttressed by the descriptive approach to language and experience of Ludwig Wittgenstein. Both philosophers emphasize the pre-reflective or "grammatical"[1] nature of experience. Husserl states it thus:

> Language has not only physiological and cultural-historical, but also apriori foundations. These last concern the essential meaning-forms and apriori laws of their combinations and modifications, and no language is thinkable which would not be essentially determined by this apriori.[2]

Likewise, Wittgenstein states that "Grammar tells us what kind of object anything is."[3]

My reflection on the grammar of fear reveals that fear always takes an object, even if the object is not readily known. Thus, I have reconsidered the putative experience of objectless fear, which is commonly called anxiety, and concluded that it is an expression of fear with a "misplaced" object. In addition, I have discovered that fear is much more than intentional; it is also dialectical. That is, it is essentially an experience which is characterized by the struggle for meaning. Therefore, fear is much more than a negative phenomenon; it is a way of interpreting the negative dynamics with a view to recovering a vision of order. As such, fear may be understood as **an interpreting experience.**

Chapter IV deals with the ways in which the dialectic of

fear is modalized. The focus here is that fear is a very intimate, though threatening, way of being oriented toward the world, and that our personalities are revealed *through*, *in*, *by*, and *with* the ways we fear. Thus, fear is much more than a response to the world; it is a kind of self-disclosure of the ego bereft of the usual garments of protection.

The reduction of fear to this (post-Edenic-like) level of vulnerability provides an opportunity for the discussion of evil. Here the concern rests with the conditions for judging any phenomenon as evil. For example, can there be an evil state of affairs without human consciousness, and is there anything more to the phenomena we call evil than their threats to our sense of order and well-being? These and other related matters are pursued in Chapters V and VI.

It is important to note that this work does not claim to answer the puzzles associated with the perennial problem of evil. Its claims are modest, but I believe they are important. One often discovers upon reflection that many of "the puzzles" associated with the problem of evil are due, not only to the way the questions are posed but, to a misapplication of categories. I have therefore suggested that the term evil is part of a religious "form of life" and that this gives it a limited secular range. However, there seems to be a strong "family resemblance" between the secular and the religious expressions of life's troubling experiences, namely, fear and evil.

These two expressions—the secular and the religious—are further examples of the two faces of fear.[4] However, whereas the secular approach sees the future in terms of the past and present, the religious sees the present in terms of a future hope which began in the past. The one devises ways of managing fears, while the other seeks ways of transforming fear into **faith-seeking-understanding**.

Finally, a word about the text and the bibliography. First, stylistically, fear and the language which relates it to evil appear to occupy more space than evil itself. This is not only to make a convincing case that fear is more pervasive than evil, but also to underscore the belief that people may have more personal experiences of fear than of evil. Besides, the process by which one arrives at an awareness of evil, if properly assessed, is learned rather than immediately experienced. In any case, we believe that the methodology of this study, which introduces ideas from Husserl and Wittgenstein, can benefit the readers who may fear delving into the sometimes forbidding prose of Husserl and the epigrammatic utterances of Wittgenstein. Thus, fear as an ongoing experience serves as a bridge both to these philosophers as well as to the problem of evil. Of course, it will be noticed that the text is evenly balanced among method (language/grammar), fear (experience) and evil (interpretation).

I have used a simple method of organizing the materials in the bibliography so that the reader can readily identify the general sources associated with subject headings. Nevertheless, I have listed all the articles in one section (without thematic organization) for no other reason than stylistic preference. It is hoped that this text will be read critically and constructively and thereby initiate an engagement of ideas and persons...The author, if not the readers and ideas, stands to grow as a result of this process.

NOTES

1. As will be made clear in Chapter III, "grammar" is a
    peculiar Wittgensteinian locution (which is also used by
    Husserl) which deals with semantics and order of
    experience rather than syntax.

2. Edmund Husserl, *The Logical Investigations*, trans. J. N.
    Findlay (London: Routledge & Kegan Paul, 1970), p. 525.

3. Ludwig Wittgenstein, *Philosophical Investigations* (Oxford:
    Basil Blackwell, 1958), sec. 373.

4. While we do not want to set up any superficial distinctions
    between the religious and the non-religious life, we feel
    that these distinctions serve to show that there is more at
    stake than one's discomfort when the term evil is used in
    religious communities.

CHAPTER I

EXPERIENCE AND INTERPRETATION

Methodological Analysis

It is reasonable to expect that anyone who embarks on the study of a problem will have a set of objectives in mind. This expectation is not only useful for the author, but necessary for the readers, who must not wait too long in discovering these objectives. It is the objective—declared or undeclared—of a study which informs its methodology. Some studies are simply summaries of past efforts in a field—and these are by no means unimportant. Others give a historical development of a problem, and/or define the limits of a field, and then pose questions about where and how we should proceed. A few make an effort to break new ground by making bold claims with, or without, adequate evidence. Finally, there are those which simply take an old problem and present it in a "new" way. That is, by considering a problem, not only with new categories but, with its elements rearranged. This rearrangement offers a new focus—a new way of "seeing."

This investigation will pursue the last-named method in the study of the problem of evil. We propose to ground the problem *in* experience and thereby see how evil arises.

To do this, we will first need to determine the nature of experience *qua* experience. Besides, if everything has its origin in experience, as R. A. Mall[1] says, then we must first attend to the structure of experience for a clue to how evil arises. Of course, the locution "structure of experience" is not without its problems. For example, is it a given? If not, how is this structure determined? That is, by *what method* can one arrive at this structure, and what are the competing methodological claims? The determination of a method of viewing experience must itself arise out of the way experience presents itself. But if the way that experience presents itself is simply a matter of *prima facie* evidence, then it is anyone's judgment as to its structure.

There are those who argue that experience has fixed limits which provide the basis for verifiable judgments. On the other hand, there are those who argue that experience has no structure except that which we impose on it. The first thesis is that of objective realism, while the second reflects the thinking of subjective idealism. The one holds to the primacy of the objective world, while the other emphasizes the primacy of the conscious subject. Both of these positions, though defensible, have serious short-comings; each narrowly defines experience from a limited perspective and thereby misses its totality. Any method which does not account for the totality of experience cannot be applied to the problem of evil, if evil spans the gamut of subjectivity and objectivity. In other words, both the objects which are judged to be evil, and the judgment itself must be accounted for.

In the next sections we will present a theory of judgment and experience which, we hope, will harmonize the totality of experience. This theory will require a method by which such a harmony can be understood and effectively applied.

Experience and Judgment

It is not an altogether useless truism that every judgment involves experience. Whether one considers judgments to be expressed by assertions (speech acts), or that they are simply a matter of recognition and observation (mental acts), it seems clear that all judgments take place *in* experience and are related to objects of experience. So whatever we say or think, it is ultimately said or thought *in* and *about* experience. Even if we choose to talk about experience *simpliciter,* we are actually talking about experience as an object—an object which arises in an intentional act. However, because experience has been variously defined, particularly by philosophers, we will need to establish a working definition that accounts both for the judgments, and that about which the judgments are made. In doing so, we will avoid the bifurcation of reality which many philosophies exemplify, as well as affirm the interdependence of the subjective and the objective.

Experience has two basic elements: the objective and the subjective. However, these two aspects of experience always go together and are distinguishable only *in theory*. There has to be "a world" of objects and "a world" of subjects intentionally correlated such that neither one is explainable without the other. We believe that this understanding captures the unity of experience. Nevertheless, this alleged unity does not obviate the questions about the peculiarities of the subjective and the objective. For example, of what does the world of objects consist which makes it unique, while at the same time able to accommodate the world of subjects? Or, what does the world of subjects share with the world of objects which enables it to form true judgments about it? In short, what is the fundamental difference and agreement between subjectivity and objectivity?

Traditionally, the answer to this latter question weighed heavily in favor of one or the other. In some explanations the subject is a necessary and primary factor in experience, while the object is contingent and secondary. In other explanations the order is reversed. Those who adopt the explanation of the primacy of subjectivity have been conveniently called Idealists, while those who affirm the primacy of objects have been called Realists. Alternatively, the terms Rationalism and Empiricism have been used, respectively, to describe these positions. But all of these appellatives are often misleading since there is no uniform agreement associated with the many forms of idealism and realism, or rationalism and empiricism. These terms primarily serve to indicate the perspective from which each group views experience. However, it is not our present task to argue for or against these positions or give a conspectus of them, but to elucidate the subjective-objective dilemma.

The subject-objective dilemma is one of the most fundamental problems in the History of Philosophy, as any cursory reading will indicate. The problem is expressed in several forms and with many complexities, but the prevailing issue remains that of determining the priority of one over the other. However, in the late nineteenth century Franz Brentano gave some new insights to this old problem. In his book *Psychology from an Empirical Standpoint*, Brentano seeks to distinguish mental from physical phenomena. He argues that every act of sensory or imaginary presentation [*Vorstellung*] exemplifies the mental phenomenon, and that every *thing* which is sensed or imagined is an example of a physical phenomenon. He distinguishes presentation (*Vorstellung*) from what is presented. Included in the concept of *Vorstellung* are such phenomena as influence, conviction, opinion, doubt,...and the entire spectrum of emotions, including fear.[2] In summary, every instance of presentation, be it cognitive or emotive, is a mental phenomenon.

By contrast, a physical phenomenon is any color, shape,

sensation, etc., which one senses. That which is received by, or through, the senses is physical, but the act of its presentation is mental. Thus, there is a very close relationship between the mental and the physical; in every presentation *something* is presented. Brentano defines physical phenomena as sensible qualities; they are only a part of what phenomena are. So if phenomena are what characterize reality, and reality is what we experience, then both reality and experience are equally mental and physical.

Brentano further argues that human beings have two kinds of perception: (1) external perception through the sense organ, and (2) a form of direct inner perception. He calls the objects of both perceptions phenomena. Thus, the objects of inner perception are mental phenomena, and the objects of acts of external perception are physical phenomena. These distinguishing characteristics are part of the result of his search for a single principle that is true of all mental acts and false for all sensible qualities. The principle which he arrived at distinguished mental phenomena as **acts** which take, or are directed toward objects, and physical phenomena as **objects** which are non-directional. Thus, he calls this insight "the principle of intentionality."

Edmund Husserl, a student of Brentano, adopted and enlarged the principle of intentionality as the basis of his phenomenology. Herbert Spiegelberg notes that "...while for Brentano the 'intentional relation' meant merely the reference of our perceiving, judging, or loving acts to their perceived, judged, or loved objects, Husserl found in these acts a much richer structure."[3] From the outset, Husserl saw in the concept of intentionality the multivalent relatedness of consciousness. This intentional "versatility" of consciousness is what Husserl elaborated on in his phenomenology. That is, the many ways of having objects which make experience much more than subjective or objective. Or, as Paul Ricoeur writes

> ...there will be as many species of intentionality, as many "consciousnesses," as there are ways in which a cogito may be turned toward something, for example, toward the actual the inactual, the past, the willed, the loved, the desired, the judged, and so on. From a strictly descriptive point of view, *intentionality avoids the alternatives of realism and idealism.*[4]

In fact, one could justifiably argue that intentionality is the phenomenological principle by which Husserl reduced metaphysical issues to questions of experience. And in the final analysis, only that which is experienced is significant. Thus phenomenology, through the insight of intentionality, demonstrates that experience and meaning are co-extensive; every experience involves some degree of interpretation, though not necessarily understanding.

There are some insights worth noting from our theoretical analysis of experience and judgment. First, everything which we experience is made possible by consciousness, and consciousness reveals to experience objects-of-sense. Therefore, anything which is recognizable is that which has some sense-determination. Second, "sense" does not only inhere in objects but in the acts by which objects are presented. Thus, "sense" is not simply sensation (experience) but also semantics (meaning). This approach to meaning (sense) affirms the intentional correlation of act and object rather than the ostensive referents alone. Third, meaning ceases to be based on a fixed referent (objective realism), or on a relative perspective (subjective idealism), but includes the many perspectives, or interpretations, which characterize the horizon of our experiences. Nothing can justifiably be called an experience except that which enters into our "stream of consciousness"; that is, through an act of meaning-conferral. Thus, experience and meaning are intentionally correlated.

This understanding of experience is phenomenological. Phenomenology maintains that an adequate account of experience has to deal with how the objective and the subjective are correlated. It does appear then that objective realism and subjective idealism are blind and empty, respectively; the one affirms an object while minimizing the act by which it is presented, and the other emphasizes the act while minimizing the object to which it is intentionally related. Both approaches to experience are myopic because they lack the phenomenological insight of intentionality—which we believe to be the most inclusive approach to the study of experience.

A Case for Phenomenology

The phenomenological "turn" signals a new approach to the problem of experience and interpretation. It views the questions of experience as questions of interpretation—questions which are self-critical but compatible with experience. But how can the questions of experience be the questions of interpretation without reducing the one to the other? The answer to this question lies in the phenomenological axiom that experience is a conscious act and, as such, it is always related to a conscious being.

It is our contention that the primary questions of experience have to do with interpretation (meaning), and that both the concern with, and the act of, interpretation are peculiarities of conscious (sentient/intelligent) beings. In other words, it can be argued that interpretation is first and foremost an expression of self-understanding. Thus, we are maintaining that the most basic questions in experience have to do with subjectivity. This bears some resemblance to Husserl's principal thesis, namely, that subjectivity and objectivity coalesce in their common beginning—a beginning which is to be found in the ego. It is noteworthy then that "Husserl's purpose is . . . to understand the nature of objectivity as related to its origin in the ego."[5]

Paul Ricoeur, in his study of Husserl's phenomenology, seeks to understand Husserl's delicate balance between the demands of idealism (a demand for *a priori*) and the demands of realism (a demand for the objective in experience).[6] The success of this "delicate balance" is what places Husserl's phenomenology beyond the division of idealism and realism. It appears, therefore, that Husserl takes on a task which is both dialectical (the synthesis of objectivity and subjectivity) and reductive (the search for origins). The motive force behind the reduction is the claim that the fact-world is delivered to us clothed in one theory or another. To "see" it in its nakedness requires a systematic and continuous disrobing. The fact that this reduction can only be done by reflection does not pose a problem since it is reflection which first brought experience to expression. Besides, a careful and responsible use of reflection, bereft of theoretical preferences, will serve as a descriptive tool for seeing more clearly. What Husserl advocates here is not a Wittgensteinian rearrangement of facts, but a radical suspension (*epoché*) of the theoretical assumptions of natural science.[7] However, like Wittgenstein, Husserl is sceptical of the "bewitching" theories (pictures) which lead to a naive realism. These bewitching theories appeal to common sense, and common sense operates with a naive object-realism.

Husserl calls this common sense posture "the natural standpoint." Common sense purports to record facts rather than interpret them. But Husserl notes that it is a curious thing to record facts without interpreting them. The very act of deciding what counts as facts, and what facts to record, is itself an act of interpretation. Besides, when one examines certain common sense claims, very often they are found to have attributions of value and sentiment. For example, we sometimes declare: "It is a beautiful day," without the slightest reservation about the "objective" character of this declaration. But while the day is there to be seen, its beauty is mooted. Thus, the objective realism which this common sense posture claims is contradictory.

Erazim Kohák highlights this and other weaknesses of common sense realism and concludes that "Common sense pays little attention to its ontological status or to its conflict with the realistic assumption that only things are real. It is content to claim that that simply is 'the way it is.'"[8] The thesis of intentionality maintains that experience is always an experience of objects to which common sense attributes primary reality. What common sense fails to realize is that experience has both a thing-objectivity and a meaning-objectivity. These objects are more than facts: "[For] quite prior to any theorizing, these objects also function as endowed with meaning, and we are quite confident to grasp those meanings 'in principle.'"[9]

Husserl's analysis of the common sense claims associated with the natural standpoint is not only to show their weaknesses, but to emphasize that a science which is built on these claims must be false. For one thing, common sense realism sees the world as being "out there," but makes no distinction between physical (outer) and social (inner) reality. Again, common sense records facts as if reality were composed of particulars. Yet, this recording of facts assumes that each particular is "a type of an object which, 'in principle,' remains constant in spite of factual variations."[10] When this naive realism is carried over to the sciences, as indeed it is, a preference is shown for facts rather than for principles. But for facts to be intelligible, they must be anchored in principles.

Husserl points out that "every fact could be 'essentially' other than it is," but that "it belongs to the meaning of everything contingent that it should have essential being and therewith an Eidos to be apprehended in all its purity...[11] Our experiences consist of particulars and principles...the one being contingent and the other necessary. Principles make it possible to identify facts as related. This is the reason why Husserl claims that our direct awareness includes both the contingent particulars, and the necessary principles. So Husserl does not object to empiricism as an appeal to experience, but as an interpretation of experience. What Husserl questions is the assumption that a theory can arbitrate what should and should not count as experience, as well as the Humean conclusion that only sensory perception of particulars should do so.[12] Husserl's quarrel with empiricists arises from their alleged "hostility to principles" and their unwarranted embrace of particulars. By limiting experience to facts, empiricists neglect the eidetic principles which constitute "the ultimate source of justification for all rational statements."[13] Husserl sees the value of the empiricist demand for a grounding of experience in the facts themselves rather than in theories. However, he is critical of the naturalization of experience since experience is much more than the facts of nature. In waving aside the conceptualism which gives a thing-like character to ideas, empiricism fails to distinguish between a thing and its correlative act. James Edie writes about it thus:

> Empiricists and nominalists have always based their refutations of conceptualism on the fact that the only *real* entities are the particular, singular, individually time-bound and space-bound physical things available to sense intuition. To speak independently of ideas or thought or concepts seems equivalent to postulating the existence of "queer entities"...and empiricists have generally felt it sufficient to refute both Meinong and Husserl by accusing them of "Platonism."[14]

Edie further states that Husserl supports the principal empiricist claim that ideal entities are not real in an idealist or realist sense; they are not "of the world," only "of our experience of the world."

Husserl focuses the argument for experience beyond rationalism and empiricism. He claims that "all reality exists through the dispensing of meaning."[15] As such, experience is real to the extent that it is endorsed with sense or meaning...our experience presents itself to us as reality to the extent that it *makes sense*, that is, presents itself not simply as a brute given but as a meaningful given. Only what *makes sense—and only inasmuch as it does*—functions as real in our experience.[16] Husserl neither advocates a subjectivist claim (that things only exist when subjects give them meaning), nor a realist claim (that things have meaning in themselves) about the existence of things. He shifts the emphasis from the nature of things to *how* they are presented *in* experience. Thus he claims that reality is not in the world or in the mind but in experience. This phenomenon of experience is characterized by acts of consciousness which bestow meaning.

Since we are first aware of experience as meaning, and there are many modes of awareness—feeling, imagining, seeing, remembering, anticipating, etc.,—phenomenology seeks to describe what is known from the perspectives of how it is known. It is the modes of awareness which determine experience (and meaning) rather than the converse. Thus, there is an immediacy in conscious experience inasmuch as it is *our own* primary mode of apprehension. When we experience fear, for example, we are not simply speculating about the reality of the world which is feared; we are, in fact, experiencing the world *through* the awareness of fear. That we reflectively attribute this mode of apprehension to a theological or psychological cause is a matter of mediate judgment, not a matter of primary experience. Here, Husserl and Hume agree that there are no primary causes, only habits, expectations, and imaginations functioning as links between temporal and spatial units. These "causes" comprise our mediate judgments of experience.

Husserl writes that "Mediate Judgments...are results obtained from grounds, which themselves refer back to immediate cognition."[17] The forms of these immediate cognitions must first be studied if we wish to arrive at self-evidence; so if fear is a primary mode of awareness which we explain as evil, then in order to understand how evil arises we will first need to attend to fear in its primary mode. Primary judgments are "objects entering for the first time into the judgment as substrates,"[18] Husserl maintains. Besides, only these substrates can reveal what is original: "Original substrates are therefore individuals, individual objects, and every thinkable judgment *ultimately* refers to individual objects no matter how mediated in a variety of ways."[19] It is the self-evidence of individual objects which makes up the concept of experience; that is, experience is "a direct relation to the individual." The task of phenomenology, therefore, is the elucidation, by way of the *epoché*, of the presuppositions of all judgments. This presuppositionless inquiry draws attention to the lived experience of subjects; an experience which accounts both for particulars and patterns, objects and acts.

It is within the context of a phenomenological inquiry, therefore, that the meaning of experience is elucidated as the experience of meaning. That is, the intentional correlativity of a pre-given object comes to thematic actuality *through* a pre-reflective act of consciousness. There is no doubt in Husserl's mind that experience is primarily a matter of meaning; and that meaning is more primordially a matter of consciousness than a matter of fact. He emphasizes that

> The theory of pre-predicative experience, of precisely that which gives in advance the most original substrates in objective self-evidence, is the proper first element of the phenomenological theory of judgment. The investigation must begin with the pre-predicative consciousness of experience and, going on from there, pursue the development of self-evidence of higher levels.[20]

Thus, experience does not simply consist of what is given; it consists of the modalization of this certainty. It is our judgments that determine the world of facts, and these judgments are traceable to the conscious awareness which makes such facts possible and intelligible. Thus, the question of experience is a question of meaning, and meaning is the product of conscious acts which are intentionally related to objects.

Phenomenology offers something new and promising to the study of the problem of experience. It avoids the extremes of idealism and realism by emphasizing the intentionality of consciousness as the axis on which "the world" of experience turns. It follows then that if experience is intentional then both the objectivity and the subjectivity of experience are preserved. This approach avoids the difficulties of subjective idealism and objective realism. It also makes room for those experiences which are often called private or intuitive. An experience is thereby no less objective because it is imagined, hallucinated, or felt; these are also modes of turning toward the world.   Therefore, phenomenology, unlike Anglo-American philosophy, places the emotions alongside of cognition. Phenomenology clearly states that experience is not simply a response to an empirical object, but a co-presence of a subject with an empirical or non-empirical object. Anything which is known has to be experienced, and there are many things which are known which do not have empirical objectivity.

Secondly, phenomenology does not merely catalogue the various objects of experience but inquires into the acts which make these objects intelligible. It is a cardinal principle of phenomenology that there is a basic intelligibility to all conscious acts; every experience comes *already* interpreted. It follows then that while we might doubt the efficacy of an object, we can never justifiably doubt that we have an experience of the putative object. Descartes demonstrated this in his *Cogito ergo sum* argument.

Thus, it is the objects which are contingent, but the experience is a necessary condition for the adjudication of the objects given-to-experience. The "given" is a primary datum for empiricists, but they classify it as that which can be observed via sensation. Husserl has amplified the notion of sensation to include all conscious awarenesses, not simply public ones or private ones but all *possible* experiences. So the whole region of consciousness is the structure which phenomenology seeks to describe.

Thirdly, if reality is, in principle, no more or less than a matter of experience, then fear is no less real when imagined; for while anything can provoke fear, "the experience of being afraid has, in principle, a 'logic of its own.'"[21] The project of phenomenology is an elaboration of this recognition. It is this recognition which we will seek to amplify in the next chapter.

NOTES

1. R.A. Mall. *Experience and Reason*. (The Hague: Martinus Nijhoff, 1973), p. 104.

2. See Franz Brentano, "The Distinction Between Mental and Physical Phenomena," trans. by D.B. Terrell, from *Psychology From An Empirical Standpoint*, vol. 1, chapter 1; reprinted in *Realism and the Background of Phenomenology*, edited by Roderick Chisholm (Glencoe, Illinois: The Free Press, 1960), p. 41. Special thanks to Roderick Chisholm for permission to use this work in summary form.

3. Herbert Spiegelberg, *Doing Phenomenology* (The Hague: Martinus Nijhoff, 1975), p.4.

4. Paul Ricoeur, *Husserl: An Analysis of His Phenomenology* (Evanston: Northwestern University Press, 1967), p. 8 [Emphasis mine].

5. Edward G. Ballard, "Foreword" to Ricoeur, *Husserl: An Analysis of His Phenomenology*, p. xvi.

6. Ibid., p.xix.

7. It should be noted that while Husserl and Wittgenstein have slightly different approaches to, and descriptions of philosophical grammar, they nevertheless share a common concern for "perspicuous seeing." In this regard, there is a "family resemblance" to their philosophy of language, as

we shall see in Chapter III.

8.   Erazim Kohák, *Idea and Experience* (Chicago: The University of Chicago Press, 1978), p. 8.

9.   Ibid.

10.   Ibid., p. 13.

11.   Edmund Husserl, *Ideas*, trans. W.R. Boyce Gibson (London: Collier-Macmillan, 1969), sec. 2, p. 47.

12.   Kohák, *Idea and Experience*, p. 155.

13.   Husserl, *Ideas*, sec. 19, p. 76.

14.   James M. Edie, *Speaking and Meaning: The Phenomenology of Language* (Bloomington: The University of Indiana Press, 1976), p. 19.

15.   Husserl, *Ideas*, sec. 55, p. 152.

16.   Kohák, *Idea and Experience*, p. 103.

17.   Husserl, *Experience and Judgment*, p. 24. It is important to note that "cognition" is used as a synonym for awareness in this context.

18.   Ibid., p. 26.

19.   Ibid.

20.   Ibid., p. 27.

21.   Kohák, *Idea and Experience*, p. 20.

CHAPTER II

CATEGORIAL ANALYSES OF FEAR

In Chapter I we outlined a theory of experience which avoided the extremes of idealism and realism. We argued that experience is intentional; it is characterized by conscious acts which intend, rather than ostend, objects. This peculiar balance between consciousness and its objects safeguards the integrity of the objects intended, as well as the acts by which they are intended. Thus, experience is not exclusively characterized by objects or acts, but by a noetic-noematic correlation of both. To paraphrase Immanuel Kant, experience must neither be sensuously blind nor rationally empty. This "middle path" between the extremes of idealism and realism is not simply novel, but *real*. Its reality is most accurately presented by means of a phenomenological description of lived-experience (*Erlebnis*).[1]

In this chapter we will focus on the lived-experiences which bring fear to thematic awareness. These experiences will be studied from the perspective of individuals, their world, and their hopes for a better and enduring world. This approach shifts the focus from the objects feared to the subject who does the fearing (without minimizing the object-value of experience). In other words, we can only successfully categorize fear in relation to those who do the fearing. This "subjective turn" is by no means a narrow subjectivism. It is experiential, in that the experiences are really those of a subject. But it also goes beyond the subjective in search of the conditions of fear, rather than focusing on particular fears. As such, we propose to examine some common expressions of fear which we hope will bring the categorial significance to light.

However, in order to place our discussion in context we

will first offer some preliminary reflections on the scope of our categorial analyses and then proceed to the cases.

Preliminary Reflections

Edmund Husserl's peculiar use of the word intuition (experience) in *Ideas 1* provides us with a useful distinction between the factual experiences of fear and the categorial significations of fear. According to Kohák, Husserl offers a substitute for the two German terms for experience—Erfahrung and *Erlebnis*—which emphasizes the generic trait of experiencing (*Anschauung*). But although the factual and the categorial aspects of experience are closely related, their distinctiveness is a requirement for any hermeneutical analysis. It is for this reason that Husserl distinguishes the categories of signification from the categories of the object signified through language. He calls the first level of the category of signification the grammatical; that is, the establishment of the formal rules by which statements become meaningful.[3] Thus, experience is not simply consciousness, but intentional awareness; and all intentional acts presuppose meaning. Or as Herbert Spiegelberg puts it: "No methodical examination can begin from the proverbial scratch."[4]

One of the values of the phenomenological approach to experience is its emphasis on the primacy of consciousness. To experience anything at all one must first be conscious. But consciousness is not knowledge; it is the pre-condition for knowing. Knowledge arises through a process of reflection—"a process of bringing to awareness." Husserl maintains that intelligibility is basic to experience. Here intelligibility and consciousness are correlated: one may find the idea of "x" problematic but recognizes that there is an "x" which is experienced as such. This intrinsic intelligibility of experience is what phenomenology seeks to articulate. It does this by focusing on the principles and patterns which make particulars intelligible. This is not the function of a mere sensuous analysis since, *ipso facto*, every analysis is regulated by the formal properties (categories) by which the phenomenon comes into view. In other words, we view things as related, and all experiences are intuited ("taken-in") as intelligible wholes rather than as discrete or isolated particulars. As Marvin Farber perceptively states it:

> There must be an act which performs some service for the categorial elements of meaning as the merely sensuous perception does for the "substantial" elements of meaning. To say that categorially formed meanings find fulfillment simply means that they are related to the object itself in categorial formation. The object with these categorial forms is not merely meant, as in the case of the purely symbolic function of meanings, but is placed before our eyes in just these forms; in other words, it is not merely thought, but is intuited, or perceived.[5]

Since reflection is the process by which the categorial elements of meaning are brought to awareness, and the process through which the sensuous becomes intelligible, then we are justified in first seeking the categorial correlates of "substantial" fear. By doing so we aim to show that fear is much more than the substantial objects we claim to fear. In fact, fear now becomes the condition for the significance of these objects. As we said before, it is the intentional relationship between a subject and an object that constitutes an experience. In this regard, there can be no justifiable denial that the nature of the intention is largely determined by the subjective act. Herbert Spiegelberg puts it even more forcibly: "...it is only by the grace of the experiencing act that the experienced object receives its title of being an experience.[6]

By implication, fear arises in the subject as a way of being aware of the world. This awareness is a function of meaning inasmuch as it is intentional. We might also add that this awareness is characterized by a critical consciousness.[7] Fear signifies that there is something threateningly different about the object experienced, or about the way it is experienced.

What this discussion acknowledges then is that all primordial experiences are experiences of meaning, and that experiences of objects are thereby symbolic. Thus, referential knowledge, which derives its evidence solely from the world of objects, is *mediate*, whereas intentional knowing is "significantly" immediate. Intentional knowing underscores both the subject and object plus the self-awareness of the subject as she acts. Additionally, whenever I describe an experience, for example, fear, I "point" to the object which occasions the fear, hoping that it will symbolically represent the experience. But whereas ostention demands objects, intention requires a correlation of subject and object, and this latter act is immediately significant. Thus, we do not simply see a man pointing a gun at another, we also see a "hold-up." Very often it is the hold-up we see rather than the weapon, or the faces of the persons in question. That we are sometimes empirically incorrect in our judgments does not negate the fact that what we had was, in principle, a *real* experience.

However, we must distinguish between a reflective

awareness which is a way of experiencing the world, and one which is a way of thinking about that of which we are aware. Reflection is not always a second order activity; it is also a way of becoming aware. Reflection is a rather useful and natural way of becoming aware of lived meaning; it does not have to be arbitrary construction of meaning, according to Kohák. It is in this sense of lived meaning that the categorial signification of fear is logically prior to the sensuous experience of fear. As such, the categorial is the pre-condition of the sensuous—it is transcendental. This is the primary task of the *cogito* in every act of awareness; it makes experience possible and every possible experience is one which in intelligible.[8] It seems clear then that we carry the possibility of intelligibility around with us, and this serves as a horizon for all acts of consciousness.

The logical priority which Kohák notes in Husserl's phenomenology begins with the subject's awareness of an act, then proceeds to his awareness of himself as the subject of the act, and ends with his awareness of the experience as meaningful. However, one does not have to be aware of the experience as meaningful (in the sense of having an immediate application) to be aware of meaning (the intentional act), since all awarenesses are functions of meaning. The "I think" must accompany all our presentations, as Kant made explicit. So if experience is intrinsically intelligible, it follows that the reflective process ("of bringing to awareness") is native to experience; it brings the categorial or pre-reflective elements of meaning to awareness. Thus, what subjectivity brings to experience is the possibility of a world of meaning. Kohák therefore concludes that apart from subjectivity the world is devoid of meaning. Phenomena do not make sense by themselves (this includes the physical and the moral), they have to be grounded with the context of subjectivity.

We can agree that all experiences begin with conscious beings who have the capacity for self-reflection. A conscious being has the ability to know that he is having an experience, or has had an experience. Language becomes an important instrument in the articulation of this awareness; it affords a medium of double awareness. That is, language brings our world to us within the form of intelligibility, as well as assists us in disengaging ourselves from the fact-world through reflection. This latter feature of language makes it possible to turn to the realm of "the meant." "The experience of language is the experience of meaning par excellence; it is our route of access to the realm of "the meant," of "sense" and "signification."[9] Or, as Lothar Eley puts it: "Language is not the guiding principle of meaning...meaning is the guiding principle of language."[10]

It seems reasonable to claim not only that language is fundamental to reflective experience, but that the most elementary level of language is the subjective act of meaning-conferral. As such, the first-person subject which predicates an object has to have greater priority in any attribution of meaning than that which is predicated. For example, consider the sentence: "I feel lonely," in which we have a subject (I), an act (feel), and a "phenomenological object" (lonely). The central (and only) act is "feel," but its centrality gains coherence in relation to the subject who performs the act. The object "lonely" (more correctly, "loneliness") is secondary in this context; it completes the act, but it is not necessary for the intelligibility of the act to state what is felt, since one can feel without knowing exactly what one feels. Besides, the grammar of intentionality makes room for elliptical objects—every act has an object, declared or undeclared. Hence "feel" is the act which issues from the subject who knows that he feels something, even if he cannot articulate precisely what he feels. A phenomenological analysis of this experience would not only focus on the loneliness, but on the feeling (act) through which loneliness comes into view. In this act subject and object are related but, according to the thesis of intentionality, only subjects can perform acts. Besides, the surest acts are those performed by an active subject. This subject is the first principle of knowledge. It is to this "subject" and its experiences of fear that we shall now turn.

The Individual and Fear

When we speak of experiences of fear, in this work, we are referring to those experiences which primarily impact an individual and his world—actual and hoped for. Ordinarily, we tend to describe the experiences of fear from the perspective of the object. For example, one is first aware of the disease which threatens ones life rather than the conditions which make the disease a threat. In an effort to move from the disease to an intelligent reason for its occurrence plausible theories are proffered. Usually, a causal theory is supplied which might, or might not, help in the diagnosis and successful treatment of the disease. But the cause of a disease is not the full explanation of the fear which accompanies it. The fear is not in the disease—neither is the disease the fear—but in the person who has the disease. It is conceivable that the fear might return even if the disease goes away. Our fears are not based on things alone, but on thoughts about things *in relation to the self.* It follows, therefore, that no object can fully explain the experience of fear, or any other experience for that matter.

With this in mind, we can safely say that fear is more primary than any object which is feared. But we must also add that fear without a subject is as blind (and absurd) as fear without an object is empty. However, our primary concern is not with what is feared, but with the subject who fears. Interestingly enough, it is the same objects which one invests with meaning that, in turn, help to heighten one's fears. Ernest Becker writes that: "Man's fears are fashioned out of the ways in which he perceives the world."[11] This is an acknowledgment that fear is a result of the meaning-frame we use "to look at" the world. But fear is more than a response to the world, since a convincing case can be made that "reality and fear go together naturally."[12] In other words, a hyper-anxious man "constantly invents reasons for anxiety even where there are none."[13] Thus, it seems that fear is both a response to, as well as a way of seeing, the world.

Accordingly, the objects spoken of above are those limits or ideas by which an individual defines himself, or orients himself toward the world. We might call the sum of these objects "the horizon of identity" or the "horizon of intelligibility."[14]

Within any horizon are the poles of support (security) and threat (insecurity), coherence (meaning) and confusion (meaninglessness), and strength (power) and vulnerability (powerlessness). One does not have to be a psychologist or philosopher in order to see that the most fundamental element of any phenomenon is that by which it is invariably defined. In short, identity is the most basic category in the attribution of meaning. This is what gives *security*, *coherence*, and *power* to individuals, and what individuals need (and use) to protect themselves against *insecurity*, *meaninglessness*, and *powerlessness*.

Identity is opposed to that which is different, alien, or

simply over-powering. To be invaded by a set of strange circumstances is to be alienated from the strength and security of ones accustomed self-image.

James Carse writes that "To be a person we must exist in ...a web of connectedness with other persons."[15] So whereas identity is the strength which gives focus, internal integrity, and social connectedness to the self, alienation is the vitiation of these. Yet, there is a dialectical relationship between identity and alienation such that the alien can be accommodated, albeit through struggle and transformation.[16] It seems that all experiences, particularly those of fear, are made possible within the vortex of the dialectical (or horizonal) poles of identity and difference. What Sören Kierkegaard calls "the dialectical determinants of dread" might also be applied to fear; namely, that "Dread is a sympathetic antipathy and an antipathetic sympathy."[17] Or as Ernest Becker paraphrases it: "Man's anxiety is a function of his sheer ambiguity and of his complete powerlessness to overcome that ambiguity, to be straightforwardly an animal or an angel."[18]

We can agree then that fear is experienced by individuals at the fundamental level of conflict—the conflict between the principles which ground the self (identity), and the principles which militate against this grounding (alienation).[19]

Events alone do not constitute fear; rather, it is the interpretation of an event as a threat to identity which generates fear. Can we also say that it is the threat, or act of destabilization, which marks off an experience as evil? Not if the term evil has any meaning beyond ones personal satisfactions. There are many "good" things (like prescriptive drugs, surgery, or dental treatment) which temporarily destabilize many persons, but these are by no means evil unless by evil we mean that which is uncomfortable, or contrary to our accustomed understanding of goodwill. That we fear pain and suffering is obvious, but can we justifiably claim that one or the other is the cause of evil? Or, do we have enough warrant to claim, as Kierkegaard and many other religious thinkers do, that evil is the cause of fear? Although we will return to the question of evil in Chapter V—The Context of Evil—it might be helpful to give an idea of how evil seems to function in expressions of fear.

In general, the term evil connotes a power *over and beyond* that which secures one's self-interest. By self-interest we mean anything which an individual or community holds dear. In fact, even if a violent act is carried out against someone whom we do not know, we can, nevertheless, become horrified if it shatters our sense of order and decency. Our sense of propriety and sobriety is breached whenever those things or persons with whom we identify are violated. One only needs to observe, in support of this statement, the anger and outcry in the United States in the 70's and 80's, against the injustices meted out to Soviet Jews and Polish dissidents. But equally significant was the chilling silence by the United States government on the decades of continuing savagery inflicted on native Africans by a white minority government in South Africa.

Those with whom we identify seem to constitute our world; all others are potential threats to the order and values we know and enjoy. It is not surprising, therefore, that countries, groups, and institutions train some of their members to discredit—and sometimes destroy—those with whom they do not choose to identify. These latter persons are conveniently defined either as unimportant, or as aliens who pose a threat. This description fits those we call enemies—persons whom we think of as evil. Thus, whenever something or someone is perceived to be a threat to identity then fear is activated, and where an individual fears for his security, he seeks protection in that which is perceived to be benevolently larger than himself. In so doing, one's identity is extended into his world—the sphere in which he receives and gives meaning and recognition. Daniel Yankelovich emphasizes that "identity reaches beyond the individual: you must identify with someone or something."[20] This "someone or something" is part of the world which forms what James Carse calls, our "web of connectedness."

The Individual's World

An individual's world is that to which he consciously belongs. It is this world, chosen or inherited, which helps to determine one's sense of identity. Identity is not simply internal; it is also arrived at in relation to a world. So the world—our horizon of meaning or *Umwelt*—is the medium through which our experiences derive intelligibility, while our identity—shaped in relation to this world—is the medium through which this, or any other world, is received. In this sense, one's world becomes an extension of one's identity, and one's identity a reflection of one's world. It is for this reason that any assault on an individual's world becomes an assault on her self-image.

We can see then that the apparent circularity of the expression "The Individuals World" disappears under careful analysis. For whereas identity is shaped in relation to one's world, this world is not entirely personal—it is shared with others. According to Husserl, the intersubjectivity of a shared world "holds good for me personally," as well as, "for all other men whom I find present in my world-about-me."[21] In other words, there has to be a basis for intersubjectivity in order to "erect" a hermeneutical bridge between and among persons. The concept of world is therefore hermeneutical as well as social; it provides a context for judgments and actions. The concept of identity on the other hand, is the door into any such context. Each door into a context will reveal shared perspectives while highlighting some distinctions.

Power

The fear of losing one's distinctiveness is the fear of alienation, while the fear of losing one's context is the fear of meaninglessness which is ultimately expressed as powerlessness. Daniel Yankelovich notes that: "Power is an equally fruitful psychosocial concept, having the same ability as identity to link the individual with the world."[22] Therefore, "power cannot be intelligently discussed without referring beyond the individual to his enmeshment in the world."[23]

The book of Genesis harmonizes the notions of power and meaning discussed above. Genesis 1:26 reports that God gave mankind authority (power) over all other created life forms. This power is expressed in terms of mankind's ability to give names (meaning) to the creatures of the universe (Genesis 2:19-20). By this report, human power resides in the ability to confer meaning on the objects of experience. We cannot but notice also that Genesis 1:26 speaks of man in the plural; this indicates that power is collective, not individual. Rollo May and Hannah Arendt both agree that power is interpersonal while strength is personal.[24] May contends that power is fundamental to being; it is actualized in situations in which oppositions are overcome; it creates meaning; it is intertwined with significance; and that most of "human life can be seen as a conflict between power...and powerlessness." This collective (group) power is peculiarly expansive; it seeks wider and larger horizons. It would appear that the more power one has the more one wants, and the more one fears losing power. Thus, we are contending that the fear of powerlessness is as fundamental as the fear of losing one's identity. In fact, alienation is often viewed as a feeling of inability to influence the events and structures of one's context.[25]

Behind every exercise or contemplation of power is a motive for its implementation. This motive is one of security beyond the edge of life and death: "...if you are wrong about power, you don't get a chance to be right about anything else; and the things that happen when the organism loses its powers are a decrease of vitality and death."[26]

Stated thus, power is not as primary as the motive which gives it direct or indirect expression. In fact, the more primary category of fear (of losing identity and power) drives many beyond the borders of the world in search of enduring realities. Thus, David Hume claims that it is man's fear of death that makes belief in immortality so attractive. Religion is thereby an expression of human hopes and fears.[27] If religion is a response to fear and mortality by means of the graciousness of God's omnipotence, then there maybe some grounds for connecting fear with power and immortality. "All power is. . . sacred power, because it begins in the hunger for immortality; and it ends in the absolute subjection to people and things which represent immortality power."[28] And as Rollo May says in *Power and Innocence*: "The ultimate in impotence is death."[29]

Life and Death

Where an individual's (or a group's) world lacks the necessary power for long term security, his feelings of inadequacy (impotence) give rise to feelings of doubts and hope. Doubts about the future, and hope that it might become secure. It is not unreasonable to want to extend the determinate boundaries of actuality into the indeterminate realm of possibility. Every such extension affords a wider horizon and a greater scope for meaning. It is from the realm of the possible that symbols and metaphors derive their hermeneutical fecundity. James Carse views the experience of death not simply as an isolating or isolated phenomenon but as an occasion for the reconstitution of the connectedness of life. He states that: "The experience of death is the experience of a perceived discontinuity that robs life of its meaning. Meaning is restored only to the degree that we have been able to discern continuity in the face of death."[30]

By emphasizing the connectedness of life Carse appropriately shifts the focus from the sensuous experience of dying to the meaning of death. As Ludwig Wittgenstein also makes evident: "Death is not an event of life. Death is not lived through."[31] This awareness lends support to the argument that it is irrational to fear that which we cannot experience. However, what is important to Carse is not whether death is experienced but, that "death is important to experience." In addition, Amelie Rorty argues engagingly that: "While it is irrational to fear death, it is no less irrational to rid ourselves from such a fear. Both views are categorically valid, requiring full assent."[32] So although we cannot experience another's death or our own, we can understand what death means for us, and this is made evident through fear.

But Carse goes on to state that: "...death confronts us whenever we experience a radical threat to the continuity of our existence. Anything that causes us to see that our lives come to nothing, and are essentially meaningless, has the power of death."[33]

It can be seen then that the fear of death is a way of becoming aware of the disconnectedness in life, as well as the opportunity for re-connections. This is the sense in which Amelie Rorty defines death-fear as functional; such fears can be useful in the preservation and extension of life. Thus Rorty opines that: "What a person fears when he fears death is perhaps what he takes to be essential and prizeworthy in his life."[34]

Irrespective of what forms our fears of death take, they mirror a longing for an enduring and meaningful life.

> Whatever the agency of death, the strategy is always to go elsewhere with life, to reach for a higher willfulness that cannot be undone by the power of death. In brief, the challenge of death will be met only by taking its threatened discontinuity into a higher continuity.[35]

All enduring meanings of life have to be larger than life as we presently know it. It follows that the absolute threat of death can be cancelled out only by the affirmation of a life which is enduring. This awareness has led Ernest Becker to exclaim that: "...there will never be anything wholly secular about human fear. Man's terror is always 'holy terror'...Terror always refers to the ultimates of life and death."[36]

However, the urge to immortality is not simply a condition of death-fear, but an affirmation of life.[37] Thus, it appears that the immortality urge is common to religious and non-religious persons alike inasmuch as it is characterized by a desire for an expanding horizon of meaning. Here we are emphasizing that "life's temporal continuity is directly coordinated with meaning."[38] Clearly then, we experience life and death at the level of meaning. That is, the fear of death can become a catalyst for more life, and the fear of life an indirect critique of human finitude and ultimate insignificance. So Becker muses and concludes as follows: "Do we wonder why one of man's chief characteristics is his tortured dissatisfaction with himself, his constant self-criticism? It is the only way he has to overcome the sense of hopeless limitation inherent in his real situation."[39]

But if the experience of death is a function of our consciousness of the disconnectedness of life, as also the consciousness of the necessity for re-connections, then making new connections is the way to face our fears and *live*. However, the inability to make new connections seems to betray a fear of life. The fear of life and death is the basis of all human repressions.[40] Persons who fear life most are the ones for whom death is most terrifying. For them, life is an exercise in escaping death, rather than an exercise in death-defiance. However, no symbol, image, place, or idea can ultimately protect one from death. There is no final refuge until escape gives way to confrontation. If not, man will always run away, even from his own shadow. In other words, that which we fear most is not in the beyond or outside of us; our deepest fears are within. These fears lead us into adverse self-criticisms and eventually into self-doubt. A diminished self-image in the face of seemingly insuperable odds is quite daunting, as the following statement attests: "The fear of life and death is encapsulated in the symptom. If you feel vulnerable it is because you feel bad and inferior, not big or strong enough to face up to the terrors of the universe."[41]

The fear of life and death is therefore quite complex, and we do not presume to understand all of the psychological elements of this complexity. Besides, this is not our present task. However, the basic structure of this fear is revealed in feelings of **alienation, powerlessness**, and **insignificance**. Thus Becker's declaration is quite apt; namely, "Man does not fear extinction, but extinction *with insignificance*."[42] It is no surprise then that our institutions, ideologies, myths, and other cultural symbols are all designed—knowingly or unknowingly—to overcome isolation, impotence, and temporal insignificance. Death forces us to seek the possibility of a secure foundation for life in spite of life's disconnectedness. This is in accord with the thesis which James Carse presents in *Death and Existence: "Death, perceived as discontinuity, is not that which robs life of its meaning, but that which makes life's meaningfulness possible."*[43] Of course, we should be careful not to idealize death as a path to new life since this could lead to savagery. But death needs to be faced rather than denied. Death is at best a "paradoxical benign agent," as William V. Spanos says.[44] However, if death-fear is an expression of an immortality impulse, the occasion of the affirmation of life's web of connectedness, or the apprehension of an insignificant truncation, as we have discussed above, then what is feared is not death itself, but what it signifies. The signification of death is what we have sought to discover in our analysis, and as one might have noticed, life and death coalesce in the significance attributed by meaning-conferring beings.

The fear of death is really a fear of the *insignificance* of death. That is, no one seriously questions the inevitability of death, although we cringe at the prospect of our own death, but we fear the prospect of a meaningless existence; whether or not such a state is entirely possible is beside the point. Death is kept in the horizon of our thoughts and is brought into focus for short spells. If we fail to put it back in the horizon, we end up being morbid, timid, or simply crippled by fear. By the same token, if we deny death, then we are simply camouflaging it with layers of cosmetics. Losses bring death into focus, as does lack of meaning, as James Carse makes explicit: "The abrupt loss of meaning in life—the experience of irreparable damage to all the lines of expectation—is not the work of something like death: it is the very force of death itself."[45] And it is at this very level that many persons experience their preliminary experiences of death which subsequently prepared them for their dying.

The preparation for dying is accommodated by a categorial understanding that while death shows the truncation of life, life demands the transcendence of death. We can also say that life is expanding, comprehensive, and purposive, while death is reductive, comprehensive, and static. Thus, if we succeed in giving hermeneutical extension to the static understanding of death, then it will cease being final or reductive, and become the occasion for deeper and wider reflections. In other words, the finality of death needs to be *suspended*, and the meaning of death explored.

In the final analysis, the ambiguity of life and death, which gives rise to fear, is, in turn, given the focus of a critical consciousness of self and world. The radical suspension of death (as final) serves as a critical tool of meaning beyond the object-content of experience. In Hegelian language, fear becomes self-conscious in life-and-death issues, and points to its resolution in immortality. Or as we said before, while alienation presents a challenge to consciousness to recover the unconscious, powerlessness presents a challenge for struggle. However, in the experience of death we find that "the resolution" of fear often arises when it is given immortal wings. Finding the categories and language to describe this new awareness is the task of our next chapter.

NOTES

1. Erazim Kohák notes that the use of *Erlebnis* pre-dominates over *Erfahrung* as the general term for experience in Husserl's *Ideas 1*. He states that this usage is consistent with Husserl's purpose "to make us aware of experience as a subject's act." See Erazim Kohák *Idea and Experience*, pp. 157-58.

2. Kohák advises against confusing intuition with any extra-experiential mode of knowing; rather, intuition constitutes "the whole range of our awareness in its primordial giveness" (Ibid., p. 160). Please note that all subsequent references to Kohák's *Idea and Experience* will be noted in parantheses immediately following the reference.

3. We will deal with "the grammar of fear" in Chapter III in an effort to discover the rules by which statements about fear might be deemed meaningful.

4. Herbert Spiegelberg, "Toward a Phenomenology of Experience," *American Philosophical Quarterly* 1 (October 1964): 331.

5. Marvin Farber, *The Foundation of Phenomenology*, 2d ed. (New York: Paine-Whitman, 1962), p. 455.

6. Spiegelberg, "Toward a Phenomenology of Experience," p. 326.

7.   Marvin Farber, in agreement with Schopenhauer, emphasizes that every philosophy that is concerned with experience is reflective, but that philosophical reflection is different from other forms of reflection. Philosophical reflection seeks to correct the uncritical acceptance of what is considered "natural." Nothing must be left unexamined, including the very method of examination. This is what Husserl means by the "radical suspension" of the natural attitude.   This *critical* (reflective) examination is a continuous task; it must be undertaken again and again. Farber reminds us that the reason for this is that the uncritical view of the world "turns out to be permeated with interpretations, and with 'deposits' of meaning going back to bygone cultural periods" (*The Foundations of Phenomenology*, p. 43).

8.   In his "Afterword" to Husserl, *Experience and Judgment*, Lothar Eley writes: "The *ego-cogito* presupposes itself. But this self-presupposing precisely does not allow the ego-cogito to become known; rather it iterates the sense of sense. It is the condition of the possibility that consciousness above all determines objects and that the horizon of the determination remains in the background, i.e., that consciousness determines appearance" (Husserl, *Experience and Judgment*, p. 407).

9.   James M. Edie, *Speaking and Meaning: The Phenomenology of Language*, pp. 47-48.

10.   Lothar Eley, "Afterword" to Husserl, *Experience and*

Judgment, p. 402.

11.   Ernest Becker, *The Denial of Death* (New York: The Free Press, 1973), p. 18.

12.   Ibid., p. 17.

13.   Ibid.

14.   In his "Afterword" to Husserl, *Experience and Judgment*, Lothar Eley states that "it is precisely this horizon, as *sense of sense*, which comes to be expressed in language." He further notes that in Husserl's *Experience and Judgment* "language is thus not only *elucidation and communication, but...*, it is that *horizon in which sense is reflected as sense*" (p. 403).

15.   James P. Carse, *Death and Existence* (New York: John Wiley & Sons, 1980), p. 4.

16.   Again, Lothar Eley notes that the dialectical is a function of language in Husserl but that Husserl did not give it explicit expression. If he had, Eley opines, he would have noted that: "*The circle of the ego-cogito and the foreconception is the prerequisite of the fact that language can iterate sense as sense*" (p. 407).

17.   Sören Kierkegaard, *The Concept of Dread*, trans. with an Introduction and Notes by Walter Lowrie (Princeton: Princeton University Press, 1957), p. 69.

18. Ernest Becker, *The Denial of Death*, p. 69.

19. Ernest Becker discusses heroism under the headings of transference, and creativity. He concludes that one form of heroism—the creative—is an affirmation of meaning in spite of extreme isolation. (*The Denial of Death*, p. 171).

20. Daniel Yankelovich, "Power and the Two Revolutions," in *The Dynamics of Power*, Jules H. Messerman, ed. (New York: Grune & Stratton, 1972), p. 106.

21. Edmund Husserl, *Ideas: General Introduction to Phenomenology*, trans. W. R. Boyce Gibson (London: George Allen & Unwin, 1931), vol. 1, sec. 29, p. 95.

22. Daniel Yankelovich, in *The Dynamics of Power*, p. 106.

23. Ibid., p. 107.

24. Rollo May, *Power and Innocence* (New York: Dell Publishing Company, 1972); and Hannah Arendt, *The Human Condition* (Chicago: The University of Chicago Press, 1958), pp. 200-1.

25. Ernest Becker, *Escape from Evil*, p. 46.

26. Richard Schacht, *Alienation* (London: George Allen & Unwin, 1971), p. 166.

27. David Hume, *Dialogues Concerning Natural Religion*,

edited with an Introduction by Henry D. Aiken (New York: Hafner Publishing Company, 1969), p. 92.

28.   Ernest Becker, *Escape from Evil*, p. 49.

29.   Rollo May, *Power and Innocence*, (New York: Dell Publishing Company, 1972), p. 40.

30.   James Carse, *Death and Existence*, p. 214.

31.   Ludwig Wittgenstein, *Tractatus Logico-Philosophicus* (London: Routledge & Kegan Paul; reprinted, 1971), sec. 6.

32.   Amelie O. Rorty, "Fearing Death," *Philosophy* 58 (April 1983): 176.

33.   James Carse, *Death and Existence*, p. 214.

34.   Amelie Rorty, "Fearing Death," p. 176.

35.   James Carse, *Death and Existence*, p. 8.

36.   Ernest Becker, *The Denial of Death*, p. 150.

37.   Ibid., p. 152.

38.   James Carse, *Death and Existence*, p. 5.

39.   Ernest Becker, *The Denial of Death*, p. 154.

40. Ibid., p. 180.

41. Ibid.

42. Ernest Becker, *Escape from Evil*, p. 4.

43. James Carse, *Death and Existence*, p. 9.

44. William V. Spanos, *A Casebook on Existentialism* (New York: Thomas Y. Crowell Company, 1966), p. 13.

45. James Carse, *Death and Existence*, p. 9.

CHAPTER III

TOWARD A GRAMMAR OF FEAR

Grammatical Prolegomenon

To ask the question: what is fear? is to invite an avalanche of responses—theories, personal testimonies, and case studies—to which any careful investigator will have to attend, though not without some qualifications. These responses would not by themselves explain fear, unless some unity could be found which holds them together. Finding the Ariadnean thread which leads out of this labyrinth of information is a tedious, if not a fear-provoking task. However, failure to find this common "thread" could result in a comparative exercise which is always in search of new information. Such an investigation might be characterized as "An Unfinished Scientific Postscript" which catalogues information without, necessarily, affording *understanding*. And as Oscar Pfister puts it: "The difficulty in this process is that it has innumerable forms and that unprecedented ones are continually arising."[1]

Of course, we will argue later that every recognition, no matter how vague, is facilitated by an underlying structure of understanding. That is, that nothing enters into our experience without some "*ad*-justment"—intentionally and dialectically.

However, for the moment, we need to emphasize that no example of what is feared is exhaustive of the phenomenon of fear. Fear has to be studied also from the perspective of what makes any experience fearsome. In other words, a search for the conditions of fear will focus on *how* fear arises, rather than on particular examples of fear. Both perspectives are useful, but the study of how fear arises provides a better economy of investigation, though not without examples of fear. This methodological bi-polarity is a feature of intentionality, and the thesis of intentionality emphasizes *how* experience is constituted. Thus, the conditions of constitution are the conditions of understanding—not in the Kantian sense of categorial imposition, but in the Husserlian sense of transcendental seeing.

We propose to call the *understanding* which holds the many pieces of information together—and which this study seeks—"the grammar of fear." As such, our concern is that of discovering and describing the unifying principle(s) of the experiences of fear. In short, we need to discover the pre-conditions of fearful experiences. Whatever these conditions are, and inasmuch as they order our conscious and unconscious life, we propose to investigate how they relate experience to interpretation.

Our peculiar use of the term "grammar" is Wittgensteinian, though not without a "family resemblance" to our declared phenomenological method of inquiry. Husserlian phenomenology is primarily concerned with the search and discovery of essential structures of experience and meaning. Thus the first order of business for phenomenology is that of discovering the unifying relationship between experience and meaning. In this regard, phenomenology is a continuous search for the eidetic principles which give intelligibility (*Sinn*) to the particulars experienced. This is a descriptive, rather than a stipulative enterprise. The emphasis is not on the meaning of meaning, or on the fabrication of an ideal language (with or without emotive and axiological considerations);[2] rather, phenomenology seeks the primary experiences to which all other experiences and expressions are primordially related.

We referred to this level of primordiality in the previous

chapters as the *Lebenswelt* or life-world of subjectivity. Nicolas
F. Gier summarizes Husserl's emphasis on the *Lebenswelt* thus:

> The Lebenswelt of Husserl's *Crisis* is the product of
> the passive synthesis of operative intentionality . .
> . . It is the "only real world, the one that is actually
> given through perception, that is ever experienced
> and experienceable."[3]

Husserl characterizes the life-world as that which "constantly
functions as subsoil" for experience and reflection.[4]

Ludwig Wittgenstein's approach to philosophy bears *some*
"family resemblance" to Husserl's phenomenology, particularly his
analysis of logical grammar and his notion that language functions
as a description of the *Lebensform*. Paul Ricoeur lends support to
this level of comparison with the following statement:

> Husserl and Wittgenstein allow a certain amount of
> comparison, thanks to the parallelism of their
> development—that is, from a position in which
> ordinary language is measured on a model of ideal
> language to a description of language as it
> functions, as everyday language or as language of
> the *Lebenswelt*.[5]

However, because we need to be cautious in our comparisons, we
have used the qualifications *some* and "family resemblances" so as
not to over-simplify the extent to which they agree and differ.
Notwithstanding, even the philosophers who are most critically
hesitant in acknowledging a Husserl-Wittgenstein comparison do
see "some" relationship between Wittgenstein's grammar of
description and Husserl's interest in the descriptive grasp of
essence:

Among these critics is Herbert Spiegelberg who
cautions that: Wittgenstein's first conception of
phenomenology is not particularly new. It is
certainly in line with the conception of a descriptive
science which can be found repeatedly long before
Husserl's phenomenology. However, Wittgenstein's
insistence on purity in the sense of freedom from
scientific theories is not equally frequent and is
worth stressing. Even more remarkable is the
interest in grasping essences. At this point one may
indeed begin to think of possible relations to the
phenomenology of the Phenomenological
Movement.[6]

This shared interest in the grasping ("intuition") of essences is
what is noteworthy for our study.

Intuitions are basic to experience; they provide the
connecting links of sense. They are not simply a matter of logical
contrivance or of psychological preference; rather, they afford an
originary vision of the *eidos* of experience. In a very real sense,
intuition is *literally* a "seeing-into" the conditions of experience
rather than an extra-experiential phenomenon or an emotional
whim. Thus, in spite of Spiegelberg's useful caution, Nicholas
Gier and others agree that Husserl and Wittgenstein situate
philosophical grammar between traditional logic and psychology.[7]
That is, that philosophical grammar is neither ideal nor empirical,
but transcendental; it deals with the conditions of the possibility of
sense (Wittgenstein) or possible meaning-forms (Husserl). Thus,
while grammar arises—makes itself known—*in* experience, it does
not derive its sense *from* the contingencies of experience; rather,
grammar shows how sense is possible.

Whether or not Wittgenstein's philosophy is
phenomenological—in the sense of "The Phenomenological

Movement"—should not detract from the point under review; namely, that philosophical grammar (Wittgensteinian or Husserlian) is a most useful locution for the study of the experiences of fear. Its usefulness is borne out in the Wittgensteinian notion that "grammar tells us what kind of object anything is." So with the most general understanding of both "phenomenologies"—as the study of the necessary conditions and the multi-dimensional features of experience—we propose to show that a phenomenological study of fear will indeed reveal a grammar of fear.

One of the recurring themes of this investigation, and of phenomenology, is that meaning is not simply a function of language, but of experience. This is the point which Dagfin Føllesdal makes in his distinction between analytic and non-analytic philosophy: the one is concerned with "meanings as expressed in language," and the other with the intimate relationship between meaning and experience. He expressed the latter thus: "To sum up, any satisfactory theory of meaning must take into account how meaning is connected with the whole variety of human experience."[8]

The recognition that "meaning is connected with the whole variety of human experience" is phenomenological. Wittgenstein, like Husserl, admits this in his now famous expression: *Lebensformen* (forms of life). He states that "to imagine a language means to imagine a form of life."[9] Wittgenstein is here calling attention to the many ways in which human beings use language, as well as to the integrity and internal boundaries (limits) attendant to each community of users. A form of life is "the given"[10] in any community; it is that in and through which every phenomenon is received and judged. R. D. Rajan, in a study of Cassirer and Wittgenstein, argues that for both men "philosophy ultimately becomes phenomenological description of the forms of our lives."[11] What distinguishes one form of life from another, and still remains unique to each, is its peculiar grammar.

Wittgenstein claims that "Phenomenology is grammar, that "Essence is expressed by Grammar, and that "Grammar tells what kind of object anything is."[12] Alternatively, these three propositions might be expressed as follows: (1) If phenomenology is grammar, and grammar discloses the essence of any object, then phenomenology is the grammar of essential forms; or (2) If phenomenology is the search for essence, and grammar discloses essence, then the phenomenological search is grammatical. None of these formulations suggests a search for grammar or phenomenology, both terms are stipulatively co-extensive. The object of search is essence; the method of search is phenomenological or grammatical. Thus, phenomenology acknowledges that philosophical grammar is that through which essences are disclosed. Of course, Husserl's phenomenology encompasses much more than the grammatical; however, phenomenological grammar is a basic ingredient in Husserl's analysis of language and world.

That there is something peculiar about the claim of grammatical necessity is evident. Wittgenstein speaks of this peculiarity as "arbitrariness." He states that logical grammar does not need to be justified since its rules are the basis for meaning: "Grammar is not accountable to any reality. It is grammatical rules that determine meaning (constitute it) and so they themselves are not answerable to any meaning and to that extent are arbitrary."[13] On the other hand, Husserl places logical grammar at the fundamental level of pure meaning-forms:

> Considering the fact that in this lowest field of logic
> questions of truth, objectivity, objective possibility
> are not yet relevant, and considering too its . . .
> role of rendering intelligible the ideal essence of all
> speech as such, one might give this basic field of
> pure logic the name of pure logical grammar.[14]

He goes on to say that the possibility of logic is a function of the unity of our experience.

Lothar Eley notes the basic function of grammar in language and experience by emphasizing that language which aims at being comprehended by itself overlooks the possibility of demonstration, as well as the rules of such demonstration:

> But (apophantic) logic does grasp—as Husserl
> recognized—*one* possibility of language. Language
> which aims at expressing itself by means of itself
> must necessarily bring grammar to an end. . . . But
> on the contrary, what really belongs to language is
> what is other than it, and this is to be represented
> according to rules of grammar.[15]

Thus, like Wittgenstein, Husserl agrees that grammatical rules are fundamental, other-directed, and constitutive. In addition, grammatical rules indirectly point to the possibility of *other* rules and contexts and thereby to pluralism. Each context has its own language-game (Wittgenstein), or is characterized by a regional ontology (Husserl). Language-games and/or regional ontologies, while constituted by logical grammar, are functions of material (rather than formal) logic; they arise in and from experience—they are synthetic. One might even argue that the combination of regional and formal ontologies, or language-games and forms of life, constitute a reformulation of Kant's synthetic a priori—the only difference being Husserl's and Wittgenstein's emphasis on the *constituting* subject. Be that as it may, logical grammar is the subsoil of all judgments—regional or formal. Thus Nicolas Gier concludes that:

> . . . there is certainly a lot to be said for Robert Sokolowski's claim that "in this matter of material logic, Husserl's constitutional studies have much in common with . . . Wittgenstein's theory of language-games, regions of discourse, which have an internal logic specific to themselves . . ."[16]

It must be noted that grammar does not indicate that nothing exists outside of one's context; rather, it makes it possible to see that whatever exists, must exist for a subject. In other words, objects only have semantic significance when they come under the rules (conditions) of our form of life. The conclusion is obvious: meaning is always contextual.

Grammar is the basic structure of the *Lebenswelt* or *Lebensform*; it is that through which we are able to refer, in Husserl's words, "*Zurück zu den Sachen.*" Intentionality demonstrates how logic is related to the world of objects (material logic) as well as how it is independent of objects in its constitution of meaning (formal logic).[17] Thus, intentionality is the expression of the synthetic apriori *par excellence*. In this regard, James Edie points out that, for Husserl, the grammatical is the first level of logical reflection; it is a reflection on language apart from the world. Husserl calls this "the pure apriori (logical) grammar," or "apophantic morphology," thus distinguishing it from the study of historical languages and their grammatical descriptions.

The study of grammar, in this sense, is necessarily philosophical. Pure logical grammar . . . is, according to Husserl, the first branch of formal logic which establishes the formal grammatical rules necessary for any statement to be meaningful at all; it is prior to and independent of all questions of the formal validity and truth value of statements.[18]

Edie goes on to say that the purpose of logical grammar is that of deriving regulative laws from originary forms of judgment: "The laws of logical grammar save us from *formal nonsense* only; it is the other levels of logic which save us from contradiction and countersense."[19] Thus, we see a useful comparison here with Wittgenstein's view of grammar as the limit of sense and the recognition of nonsense. Other forms of logic will show the difference between validity and invalidity while apophantic logic—for both Wittgenstein and Husserl—shows what is meaningful and meaningless.

How then might we apply these grammatical considerations to the question of fear? Are there features to the various expressions of fear which permit fear to be brought under a rule, or are the alleged features simply the rules by which we attempt to *impose* order onto the inchoate in experience?

These questions, though rhetorical, serve to remind us of what we have said before; namely, that every experience comes to us already interpreted, and that every act of interpretation is made possible by an underlying grammar. Thus, grammar maps the limits of sense and nonsense and thereby makes every recognition an instance, or possibility, of sense. That which does not fall within limits can neither be thought nor perceived. Wittgenstein is, therefore, most perceptive when he states that "Grammar tells us what kind of object anything is." But one might just as easily pose a counter-argument thus: Any putative knowledge claim which denies nothing (substantial) can in no way assert anything (substantial) and is therefore vacuous. In other words, that which claims to deal with everything in general, and nothing in particular, does not succeed in making true claims about the world. However, such an argument would betray an understanding of the function of principles and particulars; principles constitute "the scaffolding of the world" *through which* particulars become intelligible. As such, principles, or logical grammar, say nothing about the world; rather, they make it possible to experience the world, as well as talk about it. Every experience of the world is regulated by the grammar of the life-world which we take for granted.

The grammar of any context is that through which everything is received (in memory, perception, and anticipation); it is the intelligent constitution of everything experienced and experienceable. Thus, world and language, or experience and expression, coalesce at the level of grammar—the "subsoil" of any experience *whatever*:

> "The world," in the phenomenological sense, is the ever-experienced horizon of all the objectifying acts of consciousness, experienced coherence of all the objects presented in a given regional ontology, and ultimately, the experienced concordance of the objects of all the regional ontologies within a coherent structure of experience. . . .It is our experience of the world, as the ground of any particular experience, that founds our fundamental belief (*Urdoxa*) that all perspectives, all objectifications, will ultimately be found to coalesce

in a coherent structure.[20]

This "coherent structure" is a function of logical grammar—our unthematized way of being in the world. Grammar stays in the background in order that particulars can stand in *front* of us—in our view. However, it would be self-defeating to attempt to move such particulars from their contextual roots; this would be analogous to cutting off one's head in order to look directly into one's face. Grammar is *shown* (mirrored) in particulars, but is not exhausted by the presence or absence of particulars.

The logical grammar of fear points to the possibility—or the conditions of the possibility—of any experience being fearsome. Therefore, if experience is a correlation of consciousness and its objects, and it is necessary that they be *sensibly* correlated, then grammar is the structure which makes the correlation of experience *as sense* possible. It must be noted, however, that grammar does not cease with the impairing of consciousness; it is always there-for-consciousness. This is part of the reason why Heidegger refers to the being of consciousness as *Dasein*—that which is there for (the possibility of) existence—and situates *Dasein* in the world.[21] The world is always a world-for-consciousness; a world made possible and intelligible by an underlying ground (Heidegger) or grammar (Husserl/Wittgenstein).

It can be seen then that the grammar of the world is the *significant* unity of consciousness and its objects, and that it is problematic to separate them (as the extremes of idealism and realism have shown). Therefore, grammar does not only tell us what any object is, but *how* consciousness is able to "make sense" of objects, and of itself (self-consciousness). So the shift of focus from objects to grammar is akin to a shift of focus from the pursuit of goals to the possibility and purpose of the pursuit. Of course, this shift is always temporary since grammar does not instantiate itself.   Thus, the move from particulars to patterns constitutes a phenomenological suspension (*epoché*)—a reductive exercise of seeing beyond the particulars which we have heretofore hypostatized.   The search for the grammar of fear must, therefore, begin with an analysis (or suspension) of all theoretical assumptions.   One of the areas where theoretical assumptions are rife is that of the relation between anxiety and fear.

Anxiety and Fear

If one were to catalogue the various experiences of fear, it would be discovered that there are as many fears as there are objects.[22]   This awareness has led the more empirically minded investigators to search for the "objective" nature of fear from the perspective of the objects feared.   But this approach does not advance the study of fearful experiences beyond the recognition that some objects are more feared than others, or that some people fear objects which are not feared by others.   The objects feared are thereby set aside as fear-indicators—objects about which one should be cautious, respectful, or intensely concerned.   The cataloguing of fears does little more than identify some objects as fear-indicators, or some people as being more prone to fear (certain objects) than others.   But while this recognition might have preliminary usefulness for anthropologists and psychologists, it fails to satisfy the rigor of a phenomenological analysis.   As we have already stated, it is the logical grammar, or principle, of fear which phenomenology seeks to amplify; not this or that particular fear.   Notwithstanding, any list of particular fears, if carefully analyzed, will yield another insight; namely, that fear is intentional

—it always takes an object. It is therefore *only* the intentional correlation of fearful acts and their objects which can yield insights into the conditions of fear.

Again, while it is true that people fear all sorts of objects, it is not accurate to claim that the quantification and/or qualification of objects leads to any definitive insight into the experience of fear. Thus, the practice of defining fears as big or small, weak or strong, real or imagined, while it has some usefulness, does not advance the study of fear beyond the objective. The qualifications which we place on fear-indicators (objects) are simply metaphorical extensions of objectivities; they are objects in new vestments. A rigorous eidetic analysis of fear does not arise from taxonomic convenience (generalities) but from a penetrating insight beyond all theorizings. This is partly what Wittgenstein means by the "therapy" of [re-] arrangement of focus, and what Husserl calls "clear-seeing."[23] Of no less importance is the insight which psychologists and psychiatrists use to help patients find their way back from the objects feared, to the person who does the fearing. In the final analysis then, fear is a function of subjectivity; it is a subject's act.

But what does it mean to say that fear is a subject's act? Does this not imply that fear is, in some sense, object-less?

The literature on fear abounds with qualifying distinctions between fear and anxiety, or fear and dread. For example, Sigmund Freud argues that anxiety arises in situations of danger which are reminiscent of the trauma of birth. Like Otto Rank,[24] Freud characterizes the alleged birth trauma as the loss of, or separation from, one's object of love. He concludes that: "Anxiety thus seems to be a reaction to the perception of the absence of the object, and . . . that the most basic anxiety of all, the "primal anxiety" of birth, arises in connection with separation from the mother."[25] He further defines anxiety as a feeling of expectation of what might happen, thus putting the emphasis on the horizon of "feared-fulfillment." That is, that which is anticipated is also that which is feared, although its precise form and content are not known. Anxiety is, by this account, objectless: Freud claims that it is indefinite, objectless and is best characterized as dread.

If we are correct in our claim that every experience is grounded in meaning, and that meaning is a correlate of an intending act and an intended object, then fear must also be intentional. Given this understanding, the idea of objectless fears does seem contradictory. One way to avoid this apparent contradiction is by redefining anxiety as a subconscious act which, like fear, is anchored in a grammar that "tells us what any object is." In other words, anxiety is a form of fear, albeit, with a *nebulous* object. It is a heightened awareness of a sub-conscious (indeterminate) intention; and because all sub-conscious intentions are experienced as yawning voids, a sense of dis-ease results. This is so because, at the sub-conscious level, the intending act and the intended object are temporarily lost to each other. What we experience, in this case, is the anguish of emptiness, and not the contents of the anguish. However, this experience is no less meaningful than those with *known* objects since it is not the contents of experience which afford meaning, but their underlying grammar.

Any theory of anxiety as an object-less state confuses the felt absence of objects with the non-existence of objects. It separates the unconscious from the conscious without realizing that experience, of whatever sort, is grounded in meaning, and that meaning is the product of an intending act and an intended object. Therefore, the claim that the unconscious (anxiety) is prior to the conscious (fear) is an over-simplification of developmental psychology. Every awareness, including anxious ones, is related to a meaning-frame which is fashioned in experience—past, present, and future. Past tragedies can unconsciously live with us and thereby generate anxiety about their repetition. We re-live experiences, pleasant and unpleasant, without always recognizing that we are doing so. A pleasant breeze can give us a feeling of elation without any conscious awareness that it is *correlated* with a particular happy childhood experience. In fact, there are probably as many such pleasant experiences as unpleasant ones, except that we are not as concerned with the pleasant as with the unpleasant ones. So what warrant is there to call the unpleasant ("objectless") awarenesses anxiety, without also naming the pleasant ones?

It would seem that the issue rests with how the unconscious is defined. If the unconscious is an empty region of unfulfilled emotions, then it is clearly separate from the conscious (object-filled) region. But from what perspective, other than that of consciousness, can we speak of the unconscious? Or, can we deny the fact that conscious life, as well as the unconscious, is fundamentally related to objects of sense (meaning)? What this underscores is that we can circumvent the polemics of these priority issues by beginning to talk about experience from the perspective of *meaning*. Neither the unconscious nor the conscious has any force apart from meaning, and meaning (*qua* meaning) and consciousness are co-extensive. Thus, both the conscious and the unconscious are expressed by human intelligibility in the same sense in which intelligibility functions in utterance and silence.

Objectlessness cannot function as a "steady state" which objects interrupt, unless we are thinking of a state without subjects.

There is nothing more basic for subjectivity than intentionality. It is rather peculiar, therefore, to claim that anxiety is a prior state to fear. The clue to what makes any individual anxious can only be found in the organization of that person's experience or *Lebenswelt*—a context in which subjectivity and objectivity are *significantly* and inextricably linked. Even the argument that anxiety (dread) derives its object from the guilt of original sin, or from the awesomeness of one's non-being, is a tacit agreement that anxiety is a product of one's *Lebenswelt*.

Our task is not to isolate precisely what triggers anxiety—that is a task for the psychoanalysts—but that of showing that *something* does. And since the anxious person does not have a full grasp of what he is anxious about, then the search must first be focused on the structure of the world before attempting to pass judgment on the existence or non-existence of objects. The understanding of the grammar of such a world will tell us: (1) that there are objects to be found, and (2) "what any object is." What Kierkegaard, Rollo May, and others call object-less fears are simply "indeterminate" objects. But from the natural standpoint, where objectivity and determinacy are functionally synonymous, indeterminacy often means objectlessness. However, Husserl explains that objects are not simply "out there" or "in here," but are inextricably linked with our sense of what is or is not, *anywhere*. Something has to be for there to be any experience at all; something has to-be-for-me in order for it to be significant.

Thus, the possibility of experience is vouchsafed by consciousness, and the intelligibility of experience is a function of logical grammar. Grammar provides a web of consciousness which ensures that every phenomenon is given a place or a meaning frame. It follows then that grammar figures in the entire range of experience.

The Dialectics of Fear

Kierkegaard reasons that dread consists of some dialectical determinants which are confirmed in language.[26] That which we dread commands our keenest attention, and that which is most loved is often hedged about with fears. He states that this insight is also noted by psychology; the insight that some psychological phenomena are carriers of their opposites. This insight is also confirmed by ordinary experience. For example, we are often extremely demanding, and harshest, with those we care about most; we fear losing those we love; we are more easily hurt by those closest to us; and we expect agreement in disagreements, and vice versa. In short, emotional life is characterized by continuing ambiguities and resolutions.

This is the insight which Hegel brought to bear on conscious existence—in every act of awareness there are competing opposites which are synthesized by *Geist*. The relationship between these opposites is not accidental, but *dialectical*. Thus dialectic becomes for Hegel the instrument by which reason progresses toward knowledge. But while every synthesis is a "cooperation" of opposites, it is nevertheless a continuing struggle. This continuing cycle of thesis-antithesis-synthesis characterizes reason's teleological trajectory; reason constantly struggles *for* and *against* syntheses. By this account, it seems that nothing worthwhile is ever achieved except through struggle, and that struggle is a "cooperation" of opposites.

The experiences of fear are also dialectical. In fact, they are combative; they drive us to and fro. However, our experiences of fear also provide the training (*Bildung*) necessary to orient us to the world's diversities. Dialectic shows, above all, that diversities and ambiguities are not canceled, but hermeneutically sublated. Thus the grammar of one's context functions as an interconnected network of diversities—a connectedness under the rule of understanding. In other words, grammar makes all things possible (for sense) including those things which are contradictory. "Contradiction, in other words, presupposes sense in conflict. As such it presupposes that senses on some level are already given."[27] If there are conflicts with the sense that intentions afford, then dialectic is necessary to resolve them.

Dialectic also deals with logical contradiction; that is, the validity or invalidity of declarative statements. It can be said that the laws of logic are both the critical measure of invalidity and validity, as well as the dialectical "cooperation" of reason and existence. Logic is therefore not a description of how we think, but a stipulation of how we ought to think if we do not want to be inconsistent. However, consistency finds its expression *in* experience. Dialectic is therefore a sort of gadfly; it challenges the various organizations of experience. But dialectic does not operate in a vacuum, it presupposes sense; it operates within the giveness of a context (with a grammar). Grammar is rooted in existence—our way of being in the world. And it is more than a cliché to say that the function of its roots is quite different from that of its branches. Wittgenstein puts it in perspective thus: "Grammar shows the possibility of constructing true or false propositions, but not the truth or falsehood of any particular propositions."[28]   Meaning is therefore a condition for non-contradiction: Pure logical grammar classifies meaning-forms and is concerned with "the *mere possibility* of *judgments as judgments*, without inquiry whether they are true or false, or . . . compatible or contradictory."[29]

The influence of dialectics in philosophical hermeneutics is sometimes evident in Husserl's writings. For example, Husserl distinguishes pure logical grammar (sense) from formal analytics (validity and invalidity) and thereby sets the stage for dialectics. For whereas pure logical grammar makes sense possible, it requires formal analytics as a means of ordering phenomena. Thus language functions as a mediating influence between idea and experience. Lothar Eley points to this feature of language in Husserl's phenomenology but notes that "Husserl . . . did not explicitly work it out, but he knew of the dialectic involved."[30] The dialectical feature of logical grammar is that it points beyond itself; it demonstrates that "*language can iterate sense as sense.*" So Eley correctly interprets Husserl to say that:

> The possibility of logic is the *grammar* of language.
> Language which aims at expressing itself by means
> of itself must necessarily bring grammar to an end.
> . . . Language is the dialectic of the *ego-cogito* and
> the fore-conception.[31]

Two things are immediately clear from this observation: (1) grammar deals with sense in an originary way; that is, how sense is connected to consciousness, or to the *ego-cogito*; and (2) grammar makes it possible to accommodate otherness and thereby makes coherence possible. These two features of logical grammar are made possible by intentionality. However, the second feature demonstrates the dialectical activity of intentionality; it breaks the hermeneutical circle by recognizing and affirming a world outside of the *ego-cogito*.

Dialectic therefore fecundates understanding by transforming limits into *boundaries*—as the later Wittgenstein did—and thereby establishes *contiguity* as the first step toward synthesis or apperception. For our purposes we are defining dialectics as that feature of intentionality which functions on behalf of reason, and grammar as that which provides the basis of understanding. Understanding furnishes conscious life with a horizon of expectation which can be fulfilled by a variety of intentional acts. Reason, on the other hand, is the dialectical expression of intentionality; it scouts the limits of expectation for a richer and clearer vision of experience. Gadamer characterizes the relationship between experience and expectation thus:

> Experience is a matter of multisided disillusionment based on expectation; only in this way is experience acquired. The fact that experience is pre-eminently painful and unpleasant does not really color experience black; it lets us see into the inner nature of experience. . . . Every experience runs counter to expectation if it really deserves the name experience.[32]

We can state, without conjecture, that pain, frustration, and negativity are integral parts of experience; they indicate that the grammar of our world is equipped with a horizon which can never be fully objectified. It would seem, therefore, that *expectation* is the boon and bane of the experience of meaning. This is evident in both negative and positive expectations. When we expect unpleasant things and, instead, experience pleasant ones, we celebrate our *good fortune*; and when the reverse happens, we despair in our *evil fortune*. But are the "good" and "evil" fortunes anything more than the results of a misunderstanding of the nature of one's horizon? It is not the nature of expectations that sometimes they are fulfilled, and sometimes not?

It should be obvious also that if every expectation were fulfilled then the world would be radically altered and confused. For one thing, there could neither be any individual wills nor any reality to nature, except that which a "collective will" ordains. Expectation would give way to legislation, or even worse, to a kind of soliloquy—mind talking to itself. This monolithic and conglomerative collective consciousness would thereby will itself into a solipsistic indistinction.[33] Where the power of a collective will—or any other will for that matter—completely overwhelms and negates its antitheses, then it is only a matter of time before it turns on itself. The power to control expectations is therefore the power for self-destruction. The desire for such a power is an expression of instant and continuous self-gratifications. Of course, this is an unrealizable expectation which will always issue in frustration.

Is the putative problem of evil anything more than the frustration of our expectations?—expectations which, if always granted, would result in a suicidal form of self-gratification. Reason, by means of dialectics, forces us to demur on this midas-like syndrome in favor of a combative "cooperation" of expectation and disappointment, and their attendant synthesis or transformation. As such, the dialectic of reason preserves the mystery of life without making the mysterious sacrosanct (as Kant did in his phenomena-nomena analysis of experience). Mystery—as antinomies or contradictions—serves the cause of dialectics;

without the distinguishing activity of dialectics everything would be an undifferentiated unity (Schelling) like the dark "night in which all cows are black."[34]

If we apply these reflections to the problem of fear, we will observe that the grammar of fear also leads to a dialectic of fear. For whereas the grammar of fear deals with the conditions of the experience, the dialectic of fear takes into consideration the horizon—limits, boundaries, expectations, and frustrations—of fear. Alternatively, logical grammar answers the question of "the conditions of the possibility" of sense, whereas formal analytics—like dialectic—seeks the possibility of more sense.

We saw in the previous chapter that consciousness seeks power over death by reducing death's limits to boundaries. This occasions an ever-new and enduring significance.[35] This is a function of dialectics; it constantly challenges the actual and thereby transforms it into the possible. Likewise, expectation is a way of seeking more than the present allows; it strives to transform elements of possibility into actuality. However, because no actual object can exhaust the horizon of possibilities, it follows that, at best, expectations have to be incremental. But expectations also function negatively as threats to the satisfactions of the present. These are the expectations that fill us with fear—what some theorists call anxiety. So both the negative and the positive are expected; the one we call fear, and the other hope. When we experience pleasant conditions we sometimes fear (expect) unpleasant ones, and vice versa. But we will argue below that although fear is occasioned by the expectation of the actuality of negative possibilities, it can be overcome by a positive expectation of new possibilities; that is, of possibilities becoming actual and transforming.

The neurotics who are precariously dangling from conditional "what-ifs" (to paraphrase Robert L. Dupont's colorful phraseology quoted in the April 23, 1984 edition of *Newsweek* magazine) lack the converse expectation of "what-if-nots." To stretch the metaphor, we might say that while the conditional "what-if" (more correctly, "If . . . then") is anchored by the laws of implication, the hypothetical subjunctive—"what-if/what-if-not"—is given the wings of possibilities. This is hinted at in the *Newsweek* article thus:

> A phobic [sic] is fear looking at itself in a mirror.
> It requires self-absorption of a high order to walk
> through a crowded zoo obsessed with the possibility
> that an escaped madman will break all the locks in
> the reptile house and a big snake will slither up
> your leg.[36]

A conditional expectation is contingent; it is subject to a fixed set of variables. However, it is tied by implication to its major premise in an "If . . . then" relationship. On the other hand, a subjunctive expectation, which has a more generous array of variables, can serve as a regulatory principle for new discoveries. The one waits on the future to break forth into the present, whereas the other sees the present in the light of the possibilities of the future. This latter approach takes the challenge to the future and thereby combats a passive expectation. The conflict is therefore much more than a conflict of expectation; it is also a conflict of a negatively passive, and a positively active, expectation. And because fear is intentionally and dialectically turned toward the future, the ego must create its objects instead of having them created for it by implication. This recommendation is not simply a form of subjectivism or the over-confident *will* alluded to earlier, but a dialectical synthesis of the contingent implications (the objects feared) and the *possible* expectations (the objects intended).

Dialectic thus serves to create a new state of affairs without canceling the implications or the unrealized (but not necessarily unrealizable) expectations. In some ways, dialectic underscores the existence of fear and hope. This is the opinion expressed by Socrates in Plato's *Laches*: "In our opinion the terrible and the hopeful are the things which do and do not create fear, and fear is not of the present nor of the past, but is of the future and expected evil."[37] How one looks at the present is largely a function of one's interpretation of the future, and every interpretation of the future is either hopeful or fearful. Thus, expectation is a salient feature of the grammar of fear; it shows not only how fear arises, but how it can be managed or transformed. It can be seen then that dialectic opens up the question of the interpretive modes of fear—the focus of the next chapter.

NOTES

1. Oscar Pfister, *Christianity and Fear* (New York: McMillan Company, 1948), p. 56.

2. Examples of the "stipulative" and the "ideal" approaches to language and meaning can be found, respectively, in I. A. Richards and R. G. Ogden, *The Meaning of Meaning* (London: Routledge & Kegan Paul, 1924); and A. J. Ayer, ed., *Logical Positivism* (Glencoe, Illinois: The Free Press, 1959).

3. Nicholas Gier, *Wittgenstein and Phenomenology* (Albany: The State University of New York Press, 1981), pp. 118-19.

4. Edmund Husserl, *The Crisis of European Sciences and Transcendental Phenomenology*, trans. David Carr (Evanston: Northwestern University Press, 1970), p. 124.

5. Paul Ricoeur, "Husserl and Wittgenstein on Language," in *Phenomenology and Existentialism*, edited by Edward N. Lee and Maurice Mandelbaum (Baltimore: The Johns Hopkins Press, 1967), p. 207.

6. Herbert Spiegelberg, *The Context of the Phenomenological Movement* (The Hague: Martinus Nijhoff, 1981), p. 205.

7. Nicholas Gier, *Wittgenstein and Phenomenology*, p. 99.

8.   Dagfin Føllesdal, "Meaning and Experience," in *Mind and Language*, edited by Samuel Guttenplan (Oxford: The Clarendon Press, 1975), p. 44.

9.   Wittgenstein, *Philosophical Investigations*, section 19.

10.   Ibid., p. 226.

11.   R.S. Rajan, "Cassirer and Wittgenstein," *International Philosophical Quarterly* 7 (1967):592.

12.   Ludwig Wittgenstein, "The Big Typescript," *circa* 1933, vii, quoted in Gier, p. 437; *Philosophical Investigations*, secs, 371 and 373.

13.   Ludwig Wittgenstein, *Philosophical Grammar*, edited by Anthony Kenny, trans. by Rush Rhees (Berkeley, Los Angeles: The University of California Press, 1974), sec. 10, p. 184.

14.   Husserl, *The Logical Investigations*, p. 526.

15.   Lothar Eley, "Afterword" to Husserl, *Experience and Judgment*, p. 408.

16.   Nicholas Gier, *Wittgenstein and Phenomenology*, p. 162. Robert Sokolowski *The Formation of Husserl's Concept of Constitution* (The Hague: Martinus Nijhoff, 1964), p. 212.

17.   In contrast to J. J. Katz's proposal that facts justify
        generalities, Husserl maintains that logical grammar
        enables one to refer to facts. (see J. J. Katz. "The
        Philosophical Relevance of Linguistic Theory" in *The
        Linguistic Turn*, edited by Richard Rorty, Chicago: The
        University of Chicago Press, 1970: p. 342).

18.   James Edie, *Speaking and Meaning*, p. 48.

19.   Ibid., p. 49.

20.   Ibid., p. 8.

21.   Husserl defines *Dasein* as spatio-temporal existence and
        distinguishes it from "world"—the plenum of conscious
        life. See his *Ideas: General Introduction to Pure
        Phenomenology*, trans. W. R. Boyce Gibson (London:
        Collier-Macmillan, 1962), sec. 32, p. 100.

22.   In the *Newsweek* article, "The Flight to Conquer Fear"
        (April 23, 1984), it is noted that people fear all sorts of
        things—the familiar and the unfamiliar—that some fear
        seemingly harmless objects and events, and that a peculiar
        few fear almost everything. The article claims that "even
        if you discover where the phobia came from, it doesn't get
        rid of the fear" (p. 68, column 3). It seems then that the
        discovery of the "objectivities" of fear does not give a full
        disclosure of the experience itself, or of its roots.

23.   Wittgenstein, *Philosophical Investigations*, secs. 113, 133. Husserl, *Ideas: General Introduction to Pure Phenomenology*, sec. 19.

24.   Otto Rank, *The Trauma of Birth* (New York: Harcourt Brace & Co., 1929).

25.   Sigmund Freud, *The Problem of Anxiety* (New York: W. W. Norton & Company, 1936), p. 76.

26.   Kierkegaard, *The Concept of Dread*, (Princeton: Princeton University Press, 1957), p. 38.

27.   James R. Mensch, *The Question of Being in Husserl's Investigations* (The Hague: Martinus Nijhoff, 1981), p. 106.

28.   Wittgenstein, "The Big Typescript," p. 100.

29.   James Edie, *Speaking and Meaning*, p. 47.

30.   Lothar Eley, "Afterword," in Husserl, *Experience and Judgment*, p. 402.

31.   Ibid., p. 408.

32.   Hans-Georg Gadamer, *Truth and Method*, quoted in Palmer, p. 196. See also *Truth and Method*, trans. Garrett Barden and John Cumming (New York: The Crossroad Publishing Company, 1984), p. 319. However, Palmer's

translation is far more elegant than theirs.

33. Nineteenth-century German idealism shows an inordinate interest in the will-to-power. We see this in Fichte's (1762-1814) pervasive will, Schelling's (1775-1854) undifferentiated unity of subjectivity and objectivity, Hegel's (1770-1831) Mind-thinking-itself, and Nietzsche's (1844-1900) *Übermensch* and will-to-power recommendation. Of course, Karl Marx (1818-83) was the first to collectivize the will; but all of them embrace the power of the will as the surest way to realize human expectations. Whether they are talking about morality, aesthetics, history, social life (*Sittlichkeit*) or culture, their intentions coalesce in a desire to overcome and transform.

34. This is Hegel's basic critique of Schelling's alleged resolution-without-diremption. Quoted in Charles Taylor, *Hegel* (Cambridge: Cambridge University Press, 1975), p. 47, n. 2.

35. On this point, Richard Kroner states that: "Dialectic passes through contradictions as through its death, but it does not terminate in them. It converts them into being." See G. F. W. Hegel, *Early Theological Writings*, trans. T. M. Knox, with an Introduction by Richard Kroner, 4th ed. (Philadelphia: University of Pennsylvania Press, 1981), p. 53.

36. "The Flight to Conquer Fear," *Newsweek*, April 23, 1984, p. 67.

37.   Plato, *Laches*, 198[b], in *The Collected Dialogues of Plato*, edited by Edith Hamilton and Huntington Cairns (Princeton: Princeton University Press, 1980), p. 141.

CHAPTER IV

THE INTERPRETIVE MODES OF FEAR

In this chapter we will pursue three important vectors of the phenomenology of fear—terror, obsession and courage—in an attempt to develop a hermeneutic of fear. Parallels will be drawn between Husserl's and Wittgenstein's approaches to interpretation, while keeping the modes of fear in focus. We hope to show that the interpretation of fear is more than the interpretation of an experience; that it is also an understanding of how fear is possible. As such, our study of fear is a phenomenological study of the possibility of meaning.

The investigation of the possibility of meaning deals with how anything makes sense rather than with particular meanings.[1] However, our investigation is also hermeneutical in that it seeks to extend the horizon of meaning. This extension is not limited to what is given in consciousness *alone*, but also includes the pregiven; namely, one's peculiar way of being (existence).[2] In Paul Ricoeur's terminology, this approach replaces an epistemology of interpretation with an ontology of understanding: "Understanding is thus no longer a mode of knowledge but a mode of being, the mode of that being which exists through understanding."[3] Furthermore, we propose to show that Husserl's *Lebenswelt* and Wittgenstein's *Lebensform* are parallel terms which lead to an ontology of understanding; that is, to one's peculiar way of being. Ricoeur is careful in pointing out that:

> Husserl's final phenomenology joins its critique of objectivism to a positive problematic which clears the way for an ontology of understanding. This new problematic has as its theme the *Lebenswelt* .
> . . a level of experience anterior to the subject-

object relation.[4]

Thus, whatever we do, and however it is done, is largely a function of one's *Lebenswelt* or *Lebensform*. We will therefore demonstrate that the interpretive modes of fear are much more than perspectives or preferences; they are a subject's ways of *being*-fearful.   That is, they reveal one's peculiar self-understanding.

This ontological turn (from interpretation to self-understanding) has some important implications for the study of fear. For one thing, our modes of knowing cease to be effective if they are not also modes of being. What one knows is a function of how one understands, but how one understands is directly related to who one is. In short, we do not fear with our knowing faculties but with our entire being. To understand the ways in which one fears is to understand the one who fears; it is through these "ways" that one reveals one's self-understanding. Ricoeur writes that:

> A purely semantic elucidation remains suspended until one shows that the understanding of the multivocal or symbolic expressions is a moment of self understanding. . . . But the subject that interprets himself while interpreting signs is no longer the *cogito*:   rather, he is a being who discovers, by the exegesis of his own life, that he is placed in being before he places and possesses himself. In this way, hermeneutics would discover a manner of existing which would remain from start to finish a being-interpreted.[5]

In summary, the interpretative modes of fear are not simply ways of fearing, but ways of being. In the final analysis then,

Husserl's phenomenology can be interpreted ontologically. It has scope for an ontology of understanding in spite of its strong emphasis on the act-qualities of understanding (*noeses*). Our analysis of the vectors in the phenomenology of fear should reveal how the act-quality of fear becomes an expression of the being who fears.

Fear and Interpretation

We begin this section with the claim that fear is not simply an interpretation of an experience but *an interpreting experience.* An interpreting experience is that through which one is immediately related to the world. Through this experience, or act, the world is received and interpreted. Thus, the act of intention is itself an act of interpretation, or alternatively, objects are received as objects-meant. To a large degree, the objects which occasion fear—be they dark lonely rooms, or "haunted" mansions—are the products of our acts of symbolization. We symbolize the phenomena of experience in order to understand them and relate to them. Symbols are the means by which we orient ourselves to the world.[6]

Whether or not there are empirical grounds for fearing anything is immaterial. What is important is how persons symbolize phenomena. Thus, one might imagine a ghost and thereafter begin to run to and fro with frenzied shrieks. The experience, as constituted, would be one of fear, and *not* of an imaginary fear.

By the same token, one might walk away from a serious accident without a scratch, but becomes faint as he reflects on how close he came to dying. Our critics might argue here that this experience of fear is a product of reflection, and in some sense they would be correct. But it must be noted that the person would not simply reflect on the experience; he would be re-*living* (not repeating) it. One can reflect on an experience without being shaken by it.

However, when this reflection occasions sweaty palms, hyperventilation, or fainting spells, the reflection ceases to be a thought and becomes *a lived reality*.[7] This underscores the point (discussed in Chapter II) that reflection is both a way of becoming aware, and a way of thinking about that of which we are aware. The one is primary while the other is secondary. Notwithstanding, new awarenesses surface from second-order reflections, as is the case under review. When they do we are said to "live them."

No awareness is possible without some personal connectedness to that of which one is aware. Subjectivity brings significance to things. Thus, to say that something is fearsome is to imply that it has some significance; that is, it poses a threat. One might have experienced it before, heard others relate their experiences of it, or simply imagined its impact on one. In any case, one fears having a confrontation with it more so than one fears its mere existence. As we said above, fear is much more than a thought about something; it is an experience of the probability of coming-in-contact-with a threatening phenomenon.

Although we are able to catalogue several experiences, or things, which are potentially fearsome, it is the probable confrontation or contact with them that occasions fear. That is, only when they are likely to become experiences-for-us[8] that we become concerned. Thus, fear is always an experience *as-meant*; it is an interpreting experience.

Furthermore, as an interpreting experience, fear constitutes a way of seeing the world—and this means that fear is "a way of life." Fear is one of the many ways through which we experience the world. However, we must also acknowledge that, for many persons, knowingly or unknowingly, fear is *the* dominant way of life. These are persons who experience the world through their symbols of fear, or through their predispositions to fear. Everything takes on a part of the fear-interpreting character of their lives. These persons tend to reduce their world to certain symbols of fear—the absence of which give rise to confidence— which, in turn, function as their interpretive tools.

Technically, these symbols function as the limits of their tranquility or as their threshold. But to a lesser degree, all of us do the same.[9] For example, I have been repeatedly harassed by white policemen for driving in areas that (I am later told) are "exclusive white neighborhoods." Consequently, both the sight of a white policeman and a "white neighborhood" signify harassment to me. Of course, there is little doubt that the policemen in question have their own fears—fears which I, a black person, symbolize. However, when one multiplies these fears the product becomes a frightening scenario of evasions and collisions. But the way to avert these unsettling expressions of fear is not only to understand the world we fear, but to understand the fears through which we experience the world. These reveal something about the world that is feared as well as about the person who fears.

Interpretive Modes

1. Living in Fear

To live in fear is to experience the world as threatening

without complete confidence in averting the threats. Insecurity, vulnerability and helplessness are but a few of the descriptive terms for this state. What we described in Chapter II as the reductive, comprehensive, and static nature of death is also a part of this experience of helplessness. However, the experience of living in fear is much more than a fear of death; it is more like a fear of being alive without living, or dying without being dead. Each moment of life is no more than an opportunity for death. That is, one is kept alive in order to be tortured by the images and weapons of death. Living in fear is therefore an experience which is characterized by terror. Terrors are vigorous onslaughts against all the assurances of, and escapes to, a meaningful existence. We have witnessed this in international terrorism; no one feels secure from the terrorist's ploys. Acts of terrorism are like arrows which puncture and poison our source of buoyancy. To live in fear then is to live in a sphere of wanton recklessness from which no exits can be found.[10]

If this characterization seems harsh and overstated, it might be because we are not living in the deserts of Somalia and the Sudan, suffering from the aftermath of the poisonous gas in Chernobyl or Bhopal, India, the bombing of the World Trade Center or the Federal Building in Oklahoma, or because we have never lived in a war-torn environment like Bosnia and Rwanda. But unfortunately, these are not the only examples of terror. In an article in *New York* magazine titled "Power's Ugly Face," Kay Larson writes arrestingly about, what she calls, the "modern grammar of political terror."

Larson comments on Leon Golub's paintings which deal with the "ugliness of power." From Larson's descriptions, Golub's paintings seem to make a bold statement about the oppressive tactics of governments and their agents. Larson goes on to say that these paintings present us with vignettes of terror as executed by governments, organizations and individuals in this country and abroad.[11]

Of course, one might raise objections to the "spectacular" occurrences described by Larson with the counter-claim that they are only the product of an artistic mind. But no one, except ideological extremists, will easily object to the stories of fear and horror which the survivors and descendants of Nazi concentration camps relate. Even closer to home though, there are persons who are caught in the throes of fear—fear or escalating crime, fear of failure, fear of cancer, fear of losing one's job or of not being able to find a job, and fear of nuclear weapons in the hands of terrorists. To the extent that these fears seem imminent, and inasmuch as one feels helpless in allaying them, then one is, in fact, living in fear.

There is no denying the fact that some persons are more prone to fear than others, or that some persons fear with more intensity and longevity than others do. However, in spite of the degree of sensitivity to threats, or the intensity of fear which one exhibits, it can be said that living in fear must occasion a broken picture of life. To the extent that one experiences the world as broken one also relates to the world in brokenness. Don Ihde emphasizes that the world is a mirror for self-knowledge:

> . . . the subject, even in the Husserlian sense, does not know itself directly. Rather, it knows itself only in correlation with and through the mirror of the World. The other reveals me to myself in a way which radically modifies any naive or direct self-

knowledge.[12]

The double edge of this perception might be summarized as follows: we see ourselves in and through the world, and the world in and through ourselves. This underscores the notion of "the web of connectedness" articulated in Chapter II. Our life-world is that by which we are defined, and that to which we give definition. Yet, we are not simply a reflection of the world, neither is the world simply a matter of our creation; there is an explicit correlativity which ensures that what is mirrored is somewhat different from, yet similar to, that which mirrors. A mirror does not succeed in mirroring itself. Nevertheless, a mirror can distort what stands before it and thereby leads one to accept a false picture of herself or of the world.

For a relatively large group of persons, living in fear means a deep agony about the future; they expect the worst and therefore see the worst in everything. To the fugitive on the run the police become ubiquitous figures; to the hypochondriac, whose parents and grandparents died of cancer, every discomfort betokens cancer; and to the person who is afraid of flying, every flight puts him at the edge of death.

It can be said that one lives in fear when trust is removed. One might distrust other persons, or even nature, but when distrust turns on the self, it is the responsibility of the subject to find the means of connectedness. Without some level of connectedness there is no order, and without order there is no trust. The very foundation of civilization is based on trust—trust made possible by interpersonal give and take.

Even nature is personified as a responsive phenomenon, so as to ensure a meaningful and reasonable level of expectation. For while it is possible for the sky to fall on us it is not *reasonable* to expect this. Again, where there is no order to interpersonal relationships then expectations become nebulous, and the nebulous both blinds and chokes us. Thus, where distrust reigns, positive expectations are dashed and hopelessness sets in. Ernest Becker's exclamation that "man's terror is a holy terror" can be understood in this context as a lack of fundamental trust in the possibility of a "good" order.

Living in fear is therefore the nadir of loneliness; it is a state of interpersonal breakdown, of vulnerability, of insecurity, and a growing sense of meaninglessness. Whether one lives in the fear of the consequences of past actions (of being found out), or in the shadows of a debilitating impotence, living in fear reduces one to a mere animal. One who is bereft of basic trust is simply left with the instinct for survival. The periodic wave of vigilante action in some American cities (particularly in the 1980's) attests to this fact. Lawlessness often encourages some usually law-abiding persons to turn to crime in order to promote their sense of security and order. We can know that a society is operating at the level of the instinctual when lawlessness becomes its own justification: "I killed because I was afraid of being killed."

Life at this stage is almost automatic; one is driven by impulses rather than motivated by reason. Reason gives order to life whereas instinct simply gives it momentum. Where reason is disengaged one goes along without direction like a moving car without a driver (or without a sober driver). It is instructive to note also that living in fear can paralyze either one's will or one's reason. The one results in a total breakdown of hope, while the other slashes at everything in a self protecting-like rage. In either case, the result can be horrendous for society.

Finally, persons can learn to adjust to fearful states, but this in itself requires the discovery of a new order. The slave-master who mercilessly beats his slaves for sleeping on the job has some "order" to his behavior. However, when he beats his slaves by a lottery system (that is, simply by whim) then everyone lives in fear since there is no rhyme or reason to his actions. This is terrorizing; it is the unannounced stings from anywhere and everywhere which destroys before it kills. But even here one might successfully reason that the likelihood of his being beaten everyday is slim. This, in itself, can be a sustaining influence which helps to repress the fear.

Common sense, if nothing else, does lead us to see that "the fear of death cannot be present constantly in one's mental functioning, else the organism could not function."[13] To function while living in fear is therefore an instinctive act of self-preservation,[14] whereas, not to function is to experience a mental or physical collapse. Those who survive the terrors of living in fear are therefore those whose wills enable them to turn fear to their advantage. These are persons who live *by* fear.

2. Living by Fear

The movement from living in fear to living by fear is a complex one. It takes much more than a decision to effect this change. In fact, the fear is not removed, only its vector. Instead of tackling a stormy head-wind one turns around, or is turned around, and uses the wind to her advantage. Alternatively, we might say that living in fear is like living within an encircling gloom, which threatens to engulf us. On the other hand, living by fear comes as a result of the internalization of that which is terrifyingly encircling. This is a vertiginous experience which conduces to (and probably feeds on) our neuroses.

> The neurotic type . . . makes the reality
> surrounding him a part of his ego, which explains
> his painful relation to it. For all outside processes,
> however unmeaningful they may be in themselves,
> finally concern him. . . . he is bound up in a kind
> of magic unity with the wholeness of life around
> him much more than the adjusted type who can be
> satisfied with the role of a part within the whole.
> The neurotic type has taken into himself potentially
> the whole of reality.[15]

Thus, by this act of internalization, the circle, though unbroken, is transcended. The individual still fears, but she is no longer limited by her fears; she is driven by them.

Both the "tail-wind" and the "internalized circle" metaphors are descriptions of obsession. Obsession is a condition of being driven by something from behind or within. It is a psychological behavior that seeks to reduce the world to a symbolic unity which is easily manipulated. So whereas the cosmos is terrifying in its expanse and possibilities, the microcosmos, though formidable, is attenuated, closer at hand, and "strangely" personal. Thus, for obsessed persons, the world becomes their (re-) creation, while fear becomes the energy which keeps that world turning. The power they derive from obsessive acts grows exponentially in relation to the intensity of their fears. Were these fears removed, the obsessive neurotic would feel powerless and insignificant. The vulnerability experienced by these persons leads them to believe that there is no place which is safe from fears, and the very desire for such safety is symptomatic of the fear of life and death.

In other words, obsessive persons develop a sense of

identity, power, and significance in relation to the objects which they fear. They are in the process, not only of transcending, but of *becoming* their fears—fears of alienation, powerlessness, insignificance and death. As such, their obsessive acts show them to be agents of what they fear. There are numerous examples of this "agency theory," a few of which are worth noting.

During the late 1950s there was a growing fear of a Communist conspiracy in the United States. This fear drove Joseph McCarthy and his supporters into a Communist witch-hunt. But the very liberties which McCarthyism sought to preserve were outrageously breached in the process. The alleged communist truncation of freedom was finding expression in McCarthy's anti-communist movement. McCarthy's fanaticism about communism had led him to adopt the severe methods which Communists allegedly practiced. In like manner, the seasonal *coup d'etats* in Africa and Latin America are stark expressions of the "agency theory." Corrupt governments are overthrown only to be replaced by ones which are more corrupt and dictatorial. With each coup comes a more restricted sense of liberty and prosperity.

Another aspect of obsessive behavior can be found in the "scapegoat theory." The obsessive personality internalizes its world, refashions it, and then projects it onto others. One might even say that, "to constitute an object is to create a behavior pattern."[16] The behavior in question is that of scapegoating. Hitler practiced this in Germany and thereby persecuted millions of Jews. The personal and national inadequacies of Hitler and his Germany were conveniently blamed on the Jews. But even their firm belief in the political magic of genocide could not remove the inadequacies which were *theirs alone*, as history attests.

In like manner, though less sanguinary, almost every new

political administration blames the former administration (particularly if it is the opposite) for fiscal, foreign and domestic problems. Maybe "all is fair in love [politics] and war." But be that as it may, it can be seen that, for the obsessive, honor is not fair play, it is simply the opportunity for an advantage. Of course, it is not only politicians who scapegoat others, every compulsive person does it, particularly when threatened by failure and embarrassment.

Third, the obsessive's growing insecurity is experienced as an inward hunger for external power. Power to do things, change things, and control people, things and events. Thus, his insecurity is camouflaged by ingenuity and skill; the greater the felt need for success and power, the greater the feelings of inadequacy and insignificance. Such persons may be excellent executives but terrible associates or friends. Their demanding and uncompromising attitude, narrow principles, and impatience put pressure on everyone and everything. There is very little room for co-existence here; either one conquers or is conquered.

But this "puritanical" posture must itself lead to suicide or slow death, unless one learns to be accommodating. Because, if I need the other in order to feel powerful and secure, then the destruction of the other also becomes my destruction. This is borne out in Hegel's master-slave paradigm. The master ceases to be a master if he destroys his slaves. He has to learn to live with his slaves in a new form of consciousness—one which is not only self-preserving but other-preserving as well. Charles Taylor amplifies this aspect of Hegel's philosophy by saying that:

> men strive for recognition, for only in this way can
> they achieve integrity. But recognition must be
> mutual. The being whose recognition of me is

going to count for me must be one I recognize as human. The operation of reciprocal recognition is therefore one that we accomplish together.[17]

This is the beginning of true civility, and true civility is based on moral responsibility; that is, based on the universal rather than on the particular. Thus, Taylor argues that contradiction results

> when men at a raw and undeveloped stage of history try to wrest recognition from another without reciprocating. This is at a stage when men have not recognized themselves as universal, for to have done so is to see that recognition for me, for what I am, is recognition of man as such and therefore something that in principle should be extended to all.[18]

Finally, there is a group of obsessive persons whose low self-esteem seeks refuge in the shadow of those they admire. These are by no means aggressive persons, rather, they constantly strive to please those they fear. But the interesting thing about their admiration is that it is a cover for fear. The denial of fear is quite common among adolescents or among those who want to belong, impress others, or those who fear rejection. Quite often machismo is a transparent exhibition of the denial of fear. Freud speaks of the urge to win the favor of the father who is feared so that the fear can be neutralized. He says that

> Just as the superego is the father become impersonalized, so the dread of the castration which he threatened has become converted into indefinite social anxiety or dread of conscience. But this anxiety is insured against; the ego escapes it by

carrying out obediently the commands, the preventative measures and the penances imposed upon it.[19]

However, if the individual is impeded from carrying out these obedient acts, his fear will return with "an extremely distressing sense of discomfort," as Freud contends. This is clearly a case of fear-defense, and like the other cases, it is not a remedy for fear, only an avoidance of its immediate effects. In effect, this form of obsession is analogous to self-imposed servitude—a condition to which the feminist and black-awareness movements have pointed with scathing criticisms.[20] Neither the "uncle Toms" nor the "domesticated wives" demonstrate any recognizable sense of courage or moral responsibility.

Like those they seek to please, obsessively compliant persons seek security from their fears rather than by openly confronting them. But the fears which are hidden always become the ghosts which frighten us, especially when we are alone. The interesting thing is that while one might successfully hide one's fears, one is not so successful in controlling the symptoms which these fears occasion. In fact, he might not even be aware that fear is behind his compulsive behavior. However, the avoidance of fear, or of fear-provoking phenomena, can be very important to health. One would be quite foolish to enter a snake-pit unless she is properly protected. Or, for the youngster who has to survive on the streets in a big city, learning the rules of avoidance is an important requirement. The ability to survive anywhere is a function of knowing what to tackle and what to avoid.

Ronald Leifer argues that some forms of avoidance are necessary and rewarding:

> Avoidances . . . have a social value which is
> independent of the reality of the evil they oppose.
> They may also serve as social strategies which, for
> instance, in the form of nonviolent passive
> resistance may promote social reform, sympathy, or
> self- aggrandizement.   Or, they may serve to
> enhance the sense of mastery and self-esteem. . .
> for a job well and obediently done.[21]

In the final analysis, "The avoidance of meaninglessness is . . . the
supreme task of human life," Leifer contends.   Thus, the
avoidance of fear is a heuristic for preservation and mastery.
However, when the avoidance tactics become exaggerated, the
individual "may become so radically encrusted with self-inhibiting
and negating armor that by refusing to risk danger, he may lose
himself as a growing self-altering, participating human being."[22]
The alternative to this avoidance syndrome is that of facing one's
fears openly.   Of course, this requires both therapy and courage.
One needs a lot of *encouragement* in order to be courageous.
Whether courage is based on perceived personal strengths or on
the support of others, encouragement is an important element
thereof.

3. Living with Fear

In this section we will be presenting four postulates about
living with fear, each of which emphasizes a different aspect of
the central theme; namely, that living with fear is living
responsibly.

Paul Tillich writes that "Courage is self-affirmation 'in
spite of,' . . . nonbeing.[23]   Nonbeing, for Tillich, is the
fundamental source of all threats; it encourages despair rather than

courage. But "Courage resists despair by taking anxiety into itself."[24] What this acknowledges, according to Tillich, is that:

> He who does not succeed in taking his anxiety courageously upon himself can succeed in avoiding the extreme situation of despair by escaping into neurosis. He still affirms himself but on a limited scale. *Neurosis is the way of avoiding nonbeing by avoiding being.* . . . . He who is not capable of a powerful self-affirmation. He affirms something which is less than his essential or potential being.[25]

These penetrating insights about courage form the basis of our first postulate; namely, that *living with fear is living courageously*; it is characterized by a willingness to understand oneself in relation to or in spite of that which is troubling. Courage does not have room for excuses, subterfuges, or half-way measures—one is either courageous or not courageous. Alternatively, we might say that one either takes responsibility for oneself or is cared for by others.

However, courage is not necessarily confrontational—this in itself can be a subterfuge for a weak self-affirmation. We would like to suggest that courage is *engaging*; because even though one might tremble at the thought of his ultimate demise he can, nevertheless, struggle to stand firm in the face of its imminence. The successful removal of that which is troubling is not necessarily courageous, but the day to day engagement with it requires a quality of firmness which can only be described as courageous.

Strength of courage is not to be confused with might or force; it is more like a resolute and patient will to be, even in the face of death. As such, courage is not empty but filling and sustaining.

Our second postulate states that *living with fear is living maturely*. This can be characterized as the ability to grow in spite of negative trends. A young child has to learn to live with a sibling who constantly teases him. Wishful thinking alone will not remove a taunting person from one's experience. So before long the child learns to fight back or ignore those who constantly provoke him. The learning process here can be a remarkable index of the child's inner strengths, provided that the parents do not always interfere. By all means, a child will cry and run to a parent for shelter and solution, but an aware parent will want to encourage the child to begin dealing with his own discomforts.

Likewise, some persons are constantly exercised by troubling circumstances which can either serve to teach patience or result in self-pity. Those who learn to be patient in the midst of such struggles are persons who realize that the world is not entirely a product of personal wishes. But equally important, they are also aware that life can go on in spite of constant assaults; and it is this awareness that gives support to hope—the hope of overcoming. Notwithstanding, the desire to escape or curl up and die (which is also an escape of sorts) is quite natural. It is precisely because of this natural tendency to escape—into self-pity, complaints, etc.—why living *with* fear is so courageous. One sees and feels the crushing weight of a problem which will not go away, but refuses to die until he is, so to speak, *dead*. Courage in such cases is not simply a blind stubbornness, but the hardiness which seeks to penetrate, rather than circumvent the problem. And although this might take a very long time, as well as take one through many changes without much visible results, in the end, one is usually wiser for staying with the struggle.

This leads to our third postulate, namely, *living with fear is living with openness*. This might sound strange, but it is often the case that persons are most fearful of that which is new or different. If one expects the world to conform to one set of conditions, namely, that which does not threaten, then one cannot begin to deal with difference. Living with fear can be characterized, therefore, as a commitment (or openness) to plurality. In fact, quite often one's particularity is most threatened in contexts where plurality is shunned. The preservation of particularity is reductive and exclusive whereas the promotion of plurality is expansive and inclusive. Living with fear is therefore the ability to preserve one's roots while spreading one's branches; it is openness without total transparency.

Finally, *living with fear mirrors a synthesis of "cooperation" without cancellation*. Of course, this does not mean that one should cooperate with the symbols or agents of fear in order to live with fear. Rather, one co-exists with such forces, realizing that they are also real and that they will not go away with the wave of a magic wand. Co-existence and "cooperation" are threatening states because they signify acceptance of the seemingly unacceptable. Some of the rhetoric which came from Moscow and Washington before the 1990's suggested that political or ideological plurality was a wishful thought, and that peace could only be achieved through uniformity. Yet, common sense shows that peace is vouchsafed by mutual respect rather than by mutual hostility. Besides, neither of these two countries could have won a nuclear war; they would have destroyed each other as well as the rest of the world. Living with each other is living with the fear that one might be out-maneuvered by the other party. This is quite threatening, but not as dangerous as living in isolation from the other. Wherever there is co-existence of rival forces there will always be threats, but there will also be some elements of mutual respect and agreement.

Tillich argues that man's self-affirmation has two sides which are distinguishable but not separable. One is the self as an individualized, self-determining, and self-centered entity; the other is the world of which the self is a part. Tillich summarizes the two elements of self-affirmation as follows:

> . . . . the self is self only because it has a world, a structured universe, to which it belongs and from which it is separated at the same time. Self and world are correlated, and so are individualization and participation. For this is just what participation means: being a part of something from which one is, at the same time, separated.[26]

This is, in essence, what it means to live with fear—living in a context of fear without being overtaken by fear. Or in the more graphic imagery of the Old Testament, one can be tossed into a furnace without being consumed by it.[27]

In summary, fear is a way of understanding the world; it is both an experience and an interpretation. As such, fear is an interpreting experience, a primary way of experiencing the otherness or dissimilarities of life. In an effort to make sense of that which threatens us we symbolize the unknown in ways which give a handle to the sharp edges of life. The degree to which we are wounded by our fears is an index of the functional (or dysfunctional) value of our symbol system. A person who lives *in* fear is one whose symbol system does not work for her—she is unable to make meaningful connections.

However, the individual who succeeds in making *useful*

connections discovers new horizons, new possibilities. Admittedly, this can lead to avoidance tactics, but even these are attempts at mastering the troubling conditions of life. Mastery is a way of making things work for us and against that which threatens us. Hermeneutically, mastery can be thought of as the act of bringing something unfamiliar under the umbrella of the familiar. One of the difficulties with this approach, as Wittgenstein makes known, is that we confuse the avoidance of a phenomenon with its nonexistence.[28] That which is avoided, whether by a convenient redefinition or by some other form of symbolization, does not cease to be what it is. Obsessive persons seem to think that frenzied activity, success, or obedience are cures for their fears, but fear can only be overcome by courage. Again, this has relevance to the notion of *family resemblance*—a concept which underscores plurality. Living *with* fear is our description of living courageously, and this emphasizes, among other things, the diversity and reality of other phenomena. Thus, the relationship to fear which the courageous exhibits is an engaging cooperation. It is an attempt to understand the objects which fill one with fear, as well as the dimensions of the feelings which engender the objects as fear-provoking. There is no attempt here to define away the objects or the feelings; there are no convenient glosses for fear where courage is operative. However, the focus is shifted from the object which threatens to the self which must persist. Thus, Tillich rightly points out that courage is self-affirmation in the face of nonbeing.

Finally, we noted that there is a dialectical relationship between the subject who fears and his fear. He might be overcome by his fears and live *in* fear (terror), avoid his fears and live *by* fear (obsession), or learn to live *with* his fears (courage).

These are not simply options to be tried, but an important part of the trajectory of becoming.[29]   They show the disconnections of life, but they also point to the possibility of synthesis without cancellation.   This element of similarity in difference (or the similarity of difference) is what dialectical hermeneutics seeks. But can dialectics succeed in interpreting everything?   Are there not some experiences which defy a "happy" synthesis?

The problem of evil is a paradigm case of experiences which resist consistent explanation. Is evil then an atypical experience, or is it the limit of the rational? We will be examining the reality, character, and application of the problem of evil in the next two chapters.

NOTES

1. It must not be assumed that everyone has a unified understanding of the concept of fear. For while it is true that everyone fears, it is quite another matter to assume that everyone means the same thing by the concept. Anthony Kenny suggests three criteria for the concept of fear, any one of which is a sufficient explanation of the concept: (1) fearful circumstances; (2) symptoms of fear; (3) action taken to avoid what is feared (*Action, Emotion and Will* [London: Routledge & Kegan Paul, 1963], p. 67.)

2. Stephan Strasser, *Phenomenology and the Human Sciences*, Duquesne Studies, Psychological Series #1 (Pittsburgh: Duquesne University Press, 1963), p. 250.

3. Paul Ricoeur, *The Conflict of Interpretations*, edited by Don Ihde (Evanston: Northwestern University Press, 1974), p. 7.

4. Ibid., p. 8.

5. Ibid., p. 11. It should be noted that Ricoeur confesses to a Heideggerian interpretation of Husserl—an interpretation which finds support in Husserl's *Crisis of European Sciences* (see Ricoeur, p. 8).

6. Gordon D. Kaufman, *God the Problem* (Cambridge, Mass.: Harvard University Press, 1972), p. 101. Paul Ricoeur goes beyond Kaufman and defines a symbol as "*any*

structure of significance in which a direct, primary, literal meaning designates. . . another meaning which is indirect, secondary, and figurative and which can be apprehended only through the first" (Paul Ricoeur, *The Conflict of Interpretations*, pp. 12-13).

By this argument, the symbolization of objects is a primary function of consciousness; it symbolizies what it experiences and experiences what it symbolizes.

7.   It can be said that the awareness of the *personal* implications of an object or event (for one) is what makes anything an experience. This awareness comes with and through interpretation (symbolization). However, although we are contending that fear arises as a result of perceived threats, the absence of such threats neither means that there is no threat, nor that the experience is lacking in significance. The person who, for example, walks away unperturbed from an accident also had a significant experience. The significance which he gives to the *two* experiences is, however, quite different. And in the final analysis, is it not the significance which we give to phenomena which characterizes them as *our experience*? Erazim Kohák underscores the subjectivity of experience by stating that "reality as experience is a realm of subjectivity, meaningful in terms of a subject" (*Idea and Experience*, p. 59).

8.   By "for-us" we do not only mean that which directly applies to an individual; it also means *whoever* and *whatever* individuals hold dear. For example, an American

might not be very concerned about reports of sporadic violence in the Caribbean unless one has connections or interests there, or if one believes that this violence will seriously affect the American economy or world peace.

9. In fact, inasmuch as fear is always a part of our horizon all of us are to some degree regulated by fear. The things we attempt or avoid do have some relevance to fear. However, not everyone is *dominated* by fear.

10. That sometimes there is no empirical warrant for the experience of living in fear does not detract from the intensity of the feeling in those who fear. Living in fear is a "felt-experience" which may have "public" or "private" explanations.

11. Kay Larson, "Power's Ugly Face," *New York*, November 26, 1984, p. 116.

12. Don Ihde, Editor's Introduction to *The Conflict of Interpretations*, p. xvii.

13. Becker, *The Denial of Death*, p. 16.

14. Ibid., p. 17. There are many ways to respond to fear; one might become "frozen," run away, or stand up and fight. These are both responses as well as defenses. Our reflexes seem to take over when we are faced with dangers beyond our abilities to handle.

15.   Otto Rank, *Will, Therapy, and Truth and Reality* (New York: Knopf Publishers, 1936) pp. 146-47, quoted in Becker, *The Denial of Death*, p. 182.

16.   Ernest Becker, *The Revolution in Psychiatry* (New York: The Free Press, 1964), p. 1.

17.   Charles Taylor, *Hegel* (Cambridge: Cambridge University Press, 1975), p. 153.

18.   Ibid.

19.   Freud, p. 65.

20.   See Jacquelyn Grant's "The Sin of Servanthood," in *A Troubling In My Soul: Womanist Perspectives On Evil & Suffering*, edited by Emelie M. Townes (Maryknoll, New York: Orbis Books, 1993), pp. 199-218. This text presents a combined critique of race, gender and class discrimination as evidenced in language, theology, popular culture and institutions.

21.   Ronald Leifer, M.D., "Avoidance and Mastery: An Interactional View of Phobias," *Journal of Individual Psychology* (May 1966): 87.

22.   Ibid.

23.   Tillich, p. 66.

24. Ibid.

25. Ibid.

26. Ibid., pp. 87-88.

27. See the biblical account of Shadrach, Meshach, and Abednego (Daniel 3:20-27). One is also reminded of the burning, but unconsumed, bush which Moses witnessed on Mt. Horeb (Genesis 3:27).

28. The other difficulty is that we can re-figure the unfamiliar by means of a familiar mold and thereby exceed analogy. One needs to be on guard against attempts to minimize and marginalize difference with the contrivance of pseudo-unities. Wittgenstein's "family resemblance" metaphor is an appropriate corrective to this tendency; it underscores relationships without attempting to disregard or cancel the boundaries of difference.

29. Understanding and becoming are related functions; one understands what is different or unknown from the perspective of the known, but one's self-understanding is reflected in every act of understanding and grows therefrom. In many ways, we are both what we know and what we are capable of knowing. And as Don Ihde says, we know ourselves "only in correlation with and through the mirror of the world" (see note 12 above). According to Ihde, this is how we come to change our self-understanding.

CHAPTER V

THE CONTEXT OF EVIL

The concept of evil spans many contexts—among which are the metaphysical, the religious, the moral, and the natural—all of which coalesce in the notion of the problem of evil.[1] Each context has its peculiar assumptions and focus, but together they share the troubling sense that all is not well with finite existence. The primary awareness of this phenomenon seems to arise in the unhappy synthesis between (1) the unity we are (identity), and the disunity we experience (alienation); (2) the sense of mastery we envision (power), and the frustrations of becoming (powerlessness); (3) the hope of a meaningful and enduring future (life), and the cessation of the things we cherish (death). The problem of evil is therefore a question mark against finite existence.

It is unlikely that we would speak of a problem of evil if we could ascribe intelligent order to *all* of existence. But existence is quite complex, as the experiences we call evil attest. "Evil" is the locution we affix to the inscrutable complexities of *human* existence; it is the phenomena we do not understand, and cannot manipulate—phenomena which threaten our ways of knowing and being. However, existence by itself is neither evil nor good; it is intelligent life that determines what anything is. Thus evil, like any other phenomenon, is a problem *only* for intelligent beings. In other words, the problem of evil is one of interpretation. We might say then that evil does not arise *in* existence *simpliciter* (and certainly not *before* existence); rather, it arises *with*, and becomes a problem *for* intelligent existence. However, we must distinguish between the *being* of existence and the interpretation of existence, since existence *qua* existence is not evil.

The nature (being) of existence is a complex problem only for those who seek to fathom (interpret) and manipulate it. We are arguing then that as long as the being and the interpretation of existence are at loggerheads, evil will appear to be pervasive and inscrutable. And by extension, whatever is pervasively enigmatic is also intractable. It does not take much imagination, therefore, to see how this description of existence leads to "the problem" of evil. In fact, it always seems convenient to attach harmful qualities to that which is stubbornly puzzling and different. Thus, even the mystery of the divine—the putative source of goodness—is not exempt from the charge of evil.

But be that as it may, existence is not coextensive with evil. Evil owes its existence to the comprehensive reach of intentional life. Everything which exists gains significance in consciousness.[2] In other words, consciousness (and particularly self-consciousness) is an intelligent expression of existence. However, because evil seems to be an ongoing challenge to intelligent order, we are prone to attribute its origin to an irrational source. But evil does not arise in *existence alone*, or in *intelligence alone*; rather, it arises in the unfulfilled intentional relation of both. Alternatively, we might say that the interpretation of existence as evil results from the crushing conflicts life hurls our way. And since conflicts consist in binary opposites, rather than their parts, we must conclude that it is not the reality (being) of existence alone which is problematic, but our inability to interpret its complexity. In fact, our thesis of intentionality strongly claims that problems are exclusively expressed by intelligence—only consciousness can intend objects, objects do not take anything. Thus, "problems" are peculiarly a function of intelligence, it follows that the rationality or irrationality of existence is an expression of intelligent beings. Therefore, the problem of evil reduces to the question of how one determines the significance of existence.

We must quickly acknowledge, however, that evil is not simply "a problem" of thought but a crisis of life. The experiences which lead one to declare any phenomenon to be evil cannot be reduced to the purely conceptual. People are outraged by particular acts of injustice, perfidy, wanton destruction, untimely death, etc. These are not simply concepts but "living realities." However, because experience consists of objects and subjects—the correlation of the *noematic* and the *noetic*—it follows that the things which outrage us must also be included in, or judged by, an intelligent order. It is for this reason that we have chosen to begin by discussing "the context of evil" (rather than "the problem" or "the experiences" of evil). For one thing, no catalogue of experiences can fully describe the phenomenon of evil. Likewise, evil is much more than a logical or a theological problem; it is first and foremost a *felt* reality.

The context of evil (in contradistinction to the contexts to which we shall shortly turn) is that of the intentional correlation of experience. But there is much more at stake here than the *noetic-noematic* correlation of experience; there is also the issue of the presupposition of intelligent order (meaning). That is, where nothing is *expected* to fit together, and nothing does, there can only be aimless particulars. It would seem then that intelligent life does not begin from "scratch" but from the awareness that things (in a generic sense) matter. This is certainly the force and *raison d'etre* of the intentionality of consciousness. Thus, consciousness is both the source and the expression of meaning; it is the expression of that which it presupposes. In other words, intelligent order is a fundamental principle of experience. Whether we are talking about robots, extraterrestrial beings, exotic cultures, or ourselves, intelligent order is presupposed. That the specifics of order differ or vary is no reason to deny that the genus of existence is intelligent (purposeful) order.

Thus, whether one talks about the origin, purpose, enigma, frustration, or inevitability of evil, one cannot but acknowledge that whatever evil is, it is a problem for intelligent beings. By implication, the problem of evil is not simply a problem for philosophers and theologians, but that of the intelligent ordering of experience; and as such, it is a question of *meaning* in the broadest sense.

Yet, in spite of this general assessment, the concept of evil lacks univocity; there is no unified agreement as to what "the problem" entails. We need to look, therefore, on the contexts enunciated above to see how the problem of evil arises and is dealt with in each.

A. Evil and Metaphysics

Metaphysically, the problem of evil reduces to the question of how anything, including evil, is possible. The hermeneutical correlate of this question might be expressed thus: what is the ground or grammar of existence which allows for the intelligent attribution of phenomena? But even this question assumes *something*; namely, that there is a source from which intelligence arises, and that there are, indeed, acts of intelligent attribution which really matter. In other words, metaphysics begins with the acknowledgment that there is a reality beyond human experience which can account for all the problems we encounter. Peter R. Baelz describes this sweeping claim of metaphysics as "an attempt to overcome the incompleteness of the world by thinking it away, to find perfection where there is none."[3] However, the phenomena we call evil can neither be easily explained, nor explained away; they persist in spite of our explanations.

Richard Taylor, in *Good and Evil*, makes a convincing (and Humean) case for a re-interpretation of good and evil from the perspective of human desires and goals. According to him,

> . . . . the basic distinction between good and evil could not theoretically be drawn in a world that we imagined to be void of all life. That is, if we suppose the world to be exactly as it is except that it contains not one living thing, it seems clear that nothing in it would be good and nothing bad. It would just be a dead world, turning through space with a lifeless atmosphere.

Taylor goes on to say that unless, and until, such a world has at least one being who has feelings, desires, and goals, the question of good and evil does not arise. As he states it:

> Having deprived our imagined world of all life, we can modify it in numberless ways, but by no such modification can we ever produce the slightest hint of good or evil in it until we introduce at least one living being capable of reacting in one way or another to the world as that being finds it.[4]

It does seem then that the problem of evil is a problem of existence. But even more so, it is a problem for sentient and intelligent beings—individuals who constantly seek meaning.[5]

Thus, the metaphysical analysis of any problem, including evil, reduces to the question of meaning. However, because metaphysics seeks the primary source of meaning outside of the world of facts (a source which is unverifiable), its explanations lack descriptive value. This somewhat disqualifies metaphysics as a credible medium for the understanding of experience. In fact, according to Taylor, such metaphysical explanations introduce more questions than answers.

Like Taylor, our critique of the metaphysical analysis of evil is that it avoids the world of facts. Its rationalistic thrust seems to suggest that good and evil are givens in human experience. That is, that there are certain phenomena which are either good or evil in spite of human response. It is safe to say though that every such metaphysical analysis of evil opens up a pandora's box with a wealth of additional problems—problems which sometimes beg the question for religious answers. In this context, evil becomes a problem *before* experience arises, and, as such, it has no "solution" within experience. Notwithstanding, the problems which metaphysics raises are not entirely irrelevant; they simply need to be suspended until the questions of experience are explored. However, it is our contention that the problems of metaphysics will be refocused in the light of a phenomenology of experience.

B. Evil and Religion

Our reference to religion, while general in many ways, is limited to the Judeo-Christian tradition. We make this distinction so as to avoid the complexities of those faiths which are not theistic, as well as those which treat the Judeo-Christian "problem" of evil as a necessary part of their discipline, rather than as a phenomenon for outrage. Many Eastern religions, including Hinduism, fall in the first category, while most African religions fall in the second.[6] To tackle the complexities of each religion, *vis-à-vis* evil, would be a very complex task—one that would take us beyond the scope of this investigation. Nevertheless, it would be interesting, from the perspective of the historian of religion, to see how the different cosmologies and grammar of each give rise to the question of evil.

In general, religious assessments of evil (including the Eastern and African contexts) turn on the axis of unity and difference. But it is peculiar to the Judeo-Christian context to explain evil by a unity of which it is not a part. Biblical scholars continue to struggle with the relationship between YHWH and evil, as recorded in the Hebrew Scriptures. For the most part, many argue that YHWH is neither the originator of evil, nor does he *actively* use it. They claim instead that YHWH allows evil to befall persons or communities to (1) test their commitment (as with Job); (2) to punish them for their apostasy (Sodom and Gomorrah); (3) to demonstrate that evil would be more pervasive were it not for YHWH's divine care (Job); and (4) to demonstrate YHWH's undying love in spite of the repeated evil acts of his people (the story of Hosea).

In addition, some scholars note that the prophets and poets, in their passion for piety, did not always distinguish between what YHWH *did* and what he *allowed*. These prophets and poets saw YHWH's action and inaction as an index of his sovereign power. In this regard, YHWH was thought to be a God of wrath—what some would prefer to call his decision not to act—and a God of love. In either case, YHWH was the door through which Israel experienced anything at all. As such, he became identified with evil *without himself being evil*.

Fredrik Lindström explains that according to some scholars, there are threads of monism running through the accounts of Israel's encounter with evil. That is, the attempt by Israel's religious leaders to bring all activities associated with divinity under one umbrella.[7] There is little doubt that Israel's theological leaders were intent in showing the "economy" of YHWH, in contradistinction to the other polytheistic gods. The economy and uniqueness of YHWH is that she accommodates and contains both goodness and wrath in the divine plan of righteousness (salvation).[8]

However, whatever the intentions of Israel's prophets, poets and scribes might have been, the fact still remains that there is a phenomenon called evil. The question of where evil originally came from is still a pressing one, whether YHWH merely allows it or uses it.

We began by noting that Judeo-Christian theology turns on the axis of unity and difference, and that evil is explained by a unity of which it is not a part. But it must be noted here that every attempt to make YHWH use and/or explain evil cannot but implicate him with evil. There is no quick exit for the divine because even by bastardizing evil, the unity which sires and explains it is also called into question. In other words, unity can only succeed in explaining difference inasmuch as it is *itself* explainable by that difference. And by extension, the concept of the divine can only succeed in explaining evil if there is a *relationship* between them both. The extent to which the divine seems to be implicated in the origin and/or continuance of evil is an embarrassment to the Judeo-Christian communities. Thus, the explanation of this "relationship" is one of the basic tasks of theology; namely, *theodicy*, or the justification of the divine.

Richard Rubenstein agonizes over the nature of God (in the light of Hitler's concentration camps) and declares that it is puzzling how any Jew can believe in a good and caring God after the atrocities which the Nazi regime meeted out to the Jews.[9] Likewise, in the eighteenth century, Voltaire challenged the notion of the goodness of God after the Lisbon earthquake which killed 40,000 persons. That Voltaire was not a declared believer was no less an embarrassment for the community of faith. Today, believers and non-believers alike continue to question the alleged goodness and power of God. If God is just, powerful, and good, why does he/she *allow* the atrocities in Somalia, Rwanda, Bosnia, Oklahoma and the Middle-East?

To those who live in oppressive ghettoes theodicies are at best a poor "public relations" gimmick carried out by the initiated. Some critics argue that no theodicy can successfully protect the divine lineage from its aberrant strains. Besides, it seems far more honorable to accept one's embarrassing "relations," while trying to restrict their wanton behavior, than in disclaiming one's connection with them. Those theodicies which do the former have far more plausibility than the latter. In either case, God becomes a problem if evil exists. The existence of evil is therefore the Achilles heel of theism.

The most penetrating and sustained challenge to theism was first stated by Epicurus and reformulated by David Hume thus: Is he [God] willing to prevent evil, but not able? then is he impotent. Is he able, but not willing? then is he malevolent. Is he both able and willing? whence then is evil?[10] This challenge calls into question the logic of theism; that is, it questions the attributes of God—attributes which are contradicted by the presence of evil in the world.

Thus, it seems that the explanation of the relationship between the unity which God is, and the disunity by which evil is characterized, is still left in suspension. Those who are caught within the maelstrom of suffering, and those who cannot find a champion in God or his contrary part, are much like outsiders caught up in a family feud. In this regard, religion has its beginning in, and continues as, a quest for meaning and understanding. Whether this search is guided by reason, faith, or a combination thereof, the problem of evil assumes a meaning frame which has to be investigated. We will address this problem in the final chapter.

C. Evil and Morality

The moral assessment of evil should be distinguished from the religious, although there are some family resemblances. It begins with a gambit by which the divine is suspended in order to restore the putative purpose of, and concomitant relationship with, the divine (hypostatized as "the good"). To wit, evil is not a property of the gods, or of any personality; it is more like a parcel of land seceded from a larger estate. In order to restore unity and purpose the borders must not only be clearly drawn and policed, but every effort should be made to restore the original estate. In this regard, morality is both a limiting and a comprehensive enterprise; it prescribes limits while keeping in sight the larger vision of wholeness. Morality purports to explain and enforce right order and right relations without regard to personal endorsements.[11] We find this theme scattered throughout Plato's dialogues, among other places.

In a scintillating discussion with Euthyphro, Socrates inquired about the source and criterion of piety (righteousness) and was informed that piety is what the gods do. Recognizing that Euthyphro was reducing morality to theology, Socrates further inquired whether the gods enjoyed unanimity, and if not, by what standard should their actions be judged. Whereupon, Euthyphro replied that piety is dear to all the gods, and that they all agree that wrongdoing should be punished. However, this seemed circular and contradictory to Socrates. He is told that the gods practice piety because it pleases them. However, Euthyphro also maintains that the gods are not all pleased by the same things (they quarrel among themselves), but that they agree on the conditions and necessity of piety. To Socrates' thinking, if "pleasing to the gods" (individually and collectively) is the criterion for piety, then whatever pleases any god is piety. But unless all the gods share the same values, and never have disagreements, this definition will always be questioned. So the fact that disagreements exist among them indicates that the gods either do not know what piety is, or that the gods cannot be used as the standard for piety. In either case, Socrates maintains that piety should be loved for its own sake rather than because it is loved by the gods.[12]

However, a moral dilemma remains. That is, if good or evil is assessed without regard to those who practice it, then how does morality arise in human experience? It seems clear enough that what is judged to be good or evil is not simply a matter of personal attribution—there has to be something which exists *in correlation* with one's judgment of it. However, nothing can be judged to be good or evil except in consciousness; that is, unless it becomes a part of, or arises in, one's conscious life. It is therefore at the level of consciousness, intentionally correlated, that the moral dilemma of evil gains significance. Thus, whatever one defines as evil must have some significance for conscious life, albeit negatively. In other words, the question of evil does not arise outside of conscious life.

Richard Taylor, like Hobbes, Hume, locates the origin of good and evil in desires and aversions, interpreted as right and wrong, respectively, and therefrom distinguishes the one from the other. That is, good and evil arise in the intentional life of beings who, by definition, have wants, needs, and purpose. Moral obligation, on the other hand, arises in community life; that is, where aims or purposes are liable to collide. As Taylor states,

> . . . even though good and evil have emerged with the appearance in this world of a single living being having wants and needs, no moral obligation has similarly arisen. The distinction between moral *right* and *wrong* has not yet come into the picture.[13]

However, with the multiplicity of such beings there arises the possibility of conflict and/or cooperation.

> Thus, two or more such beings can covet the same thing. In that case each will deem it good, but it can easily arise that not both can possess it, that its possession by one will mean deprivation for the other. The result is a conflict of wills, which can lead to mutual aggression in which each stands to lose more than the thing for which they are contending is worth to either of them.[14]

Taylor concludes then that right and wrong arise against the background of conflict and cooperation which are, in turn, regulated by *rules*. As such, right and wrong are always rule governed; the one is the adherence to rules, while the other is the violation of rules. However, good and evil are attributes we place on the phenomena which satisfy or threaten our sense of purpose or well-being. We might consider it "good" to adhere to a rule, and "evil" to violate it, but this does not mean that good and evil are necessarily rule governed. Something might be adjudged to be good because it is right—it promotes cooperation—and evil because it is wrong—it promotes conflict. However, very often the breaking of a rule promotes that which is good; for example, in the overthrow of tyranny. Thus, the impasse between Socrates and Euthyphro is also ours—evil is partly what displeases, but what displeases must also fall under a rule. In other words, good and evil must also have some universal significance.

For our purposes, however, it is sufficient to note that good and evil are interpretations of the primary levels of experience. That is, the levels where satisfaction and threat (frustration) are at stake.[15] In the light of Chapter II we might add that evil is the threat to identity (security), power (cooperation), and an enduring meaning (immortality), while goodness is what underpins them. Secondly, by placing good and evil within human will (consciousness), the question of unity and difference assumes a closer (intrinsic) relationship, in contradistinction to rationalistic (extrinsic) analyses. And finally, good and evil do not have to be apotheosized, but can be dealt with as "facts" in human experience. Therefore, evil has to be tackled as a challenge to subjectivity rather than to divinity. This is so since no metaphysical or theological speculation about the origin of life can explain away the fact that humans have desires, needs, and goals. It is therefore from this subjective point—the locus of human consciousness—that the investigation of origin has to begin.

D. Evil and Nature

The logical conundrums implicit in the metaphysical, religious, and moral contexts might leave the average person in a suspended state *vis-à-vis* a plausible answer to the problem of evil. However, for many persons, the desire to explain, if not fully understand, the problem of evil moves beyond suspension and finds expression in the notion of *the abiding complexity* of nature. The justification for this approach might be summarized as follows: we are surrounded by nature, and we are a part of nature; everything which comes to us comes through the medium of nature. It would seem much easier then to understand, or at least accept, nature than the theories about how nature came to be. To try to understand evil within the context of nature (in its broadest sense) might be said to be an important first step toward self-understanding. This is so because nature is not only close at hand, but also lives in and through us. This level of intimacy with nature should not be taken for granted in the search for understanding.

The word "nature" connotes many things, but its most general understanding is that of the physical environment. However, as soon as the physical is experienced it ceases to be simply physical and receives the values of space, temporality, and use. Physical nature is not simply "there"; it is there *with* and *for* us. As a result, our descriptions of nature range from the aesthetic to the pragmatic. We celebrate the beauty of nature, enjoy its fruits, ponder its actions and inactions, lament its expressions of death, and seek ways to enlarge and harness its powers. Yet, in spite of these, nature is still puzzling.

Nature has a way of erupting in volcanoes, earthquakes,

storms and floods; it sometimes grows deathly silent in droughts (which result in famine), as well as plays hide-and-seek games with extremes in temperature. Over against these seemingly disorderly acts, nature has its "laws" of gravity, inertia, growth and decay. The sum total of these attributes might be called unity and diversity, order and disorder, or harmony and discord. It is little wonder then that "nature" has come to mean "the sum total of *everything.*" Thus, to say that something is natural is to acknowledge, among other things, that it is part of a larger order of things, and that is has no further explanation beyond our experience of it. In short, nature is self-defining; everything which is needed to understand nature can be found within. Of course, nature's complexity does lend itself to wide-ranging assessments.[16]

There are those who interpret nature's diversity in terms of a rich and promising variety, while others view this diversity as the expression of incompletion. Some seek for the patterns of nature's activities and thereby develop a science of order and expectation. But some grow weary of observation and, instead of seeking intrinsic patterns, grope for extrinsic explanations. Thus, while physics is one of the principal sciences of nature's behavior, *meta*physics (in reaching beyond the observable) purports to be the "science" of nature's origin and purpose. Both acknowledge that nature has to be interpreted, but the one seeks its explanations from the active features of nature while the other searches for the alleged "causes" of such features. We will return to these distinctions in the final chapter when we discuss evil in the light of faith and reason. Suffice it to say that nature only becomes intelligible when interpreted, or when intended by a subject.

However, the question of nature's self-validation—that is,

the intrinsic explanations based on *facts*—can be puzzling. Erazim Kohák carefully points out that experience explains facts, not vice versa.[17] That is, facts have no existence or explanatory power apart from consciousness. Thus, for a phenomenon to be deemed factual it must be open to intersubjective validation.

> But the shared reality of our world is a reality shared in experience. Thus we cannot explain the intersubjective validity of our perceptions in terms of the undenied reality of the perceived world. Our common recognition of certain contents of our experience as real presupposes a shared experience and so cannot explain it.[18]

Is there any warrant to the argument that things are the way they are? Can we not change our perceptions of things so that they assume a new form (meaning)? Of course, some persons will object to this proposal with the reminder that collective existence presupposes a history and an order of interpretation. That is, there is a recursive grammar which, though transformational, is generative. Thus, one does not begin to "make sense" from scratch with every new experience; the new is related to the old because of an underlying order or grammar.

Alternatively, we might say that every phenomenon has a place in our horizon, whether it is similar to, or different from what we have hitherto experienced. But be that as it may, there is much warrant in the explorations of the many ways of *seeing*. Things are the way they are only because intelligence orders them that way. Phenomena are experienced against an expanding horizon and, therefore, they cannot be irrevocably fixed. Neither objects (*noemata*) nor the acts (*noeses*) by which they are intended are fixed. Experience is grounded by logical grammar—the logical principles which vouchsafe order and intelligence. And even these principles are little more than arbitrary ways of regulating and describing order in experience.

When we apply this argument to the question of evil we can see that evil is related to the notion of intelligent order. All of us have a strong desire to give the phenomenon of evil an origin and a purpose simply because it is a *natural* expression of the grammar of our experience to do so. But does the problem of evil disappear when a suitable explanation is found? By no means, for as long as there are disappointments, untimely deaths, suffering and frustration, there is cause to speak of evil. However, evil does seem to lose some of its sting, though not its reality, with an "appropriate" explanation. This is partly what takes place when we are encouraged after a failure, loss or disappointment. There is a strong desire in us, it seems, for things to make sense.

Again, the question of unity and difference arises. For if evil means nothing more than one's inability to find a pattern for certain occurrences, then the locution "evil" is reduced to a critique of knowledge.[19] That is, evil is any phenomenon which is inscrutable and/or intractable. This acknowledgment can function as a challenge for new ways of understanding; or it may occasion an incurious posture: "that's the way things are." However, even this latter response is a way of dealing with what seems troubling; one simply refuses *to be troubled* unnecessarily by what one believes to be part of the order of things. But while cynics and existentialists, among others, might succeed for a while with this posture, most persons have a strong desire to understand and change things; and these are the ones for whom evil poses the greatest challenge.

On the other hand, to say in the wake of the disturbing

occurrences in nature that "this is the way things are" is to neglect one important expression of nature; namely, intelligent order. Nature is not simply neutral; its actions, inter-actions, and inactions do have consequences for intelligent beings—consequences to which consciousness gives intelligent location (spatially and temporally). For example, why did the tree not fall 15 degrees to the right or left of Jim, or five minutes before or after Jim's arrival, instead of on him? It does seem then that if there is any evil or goodness in nature it is not due to intrinsic or extrinsic properties, but to the consequences for intelligent beings.

Even the notion of pain and suffering in animals is without significance apart from human affection (provided that we continue to maintain that animals lack intelligence). If animal suffering matters to animals themselves—which it clearly does—then we must also admit that animals have some sense or order, no matter how small. But can we also say that there is no suffering within the plant kingdom? Of course, this is a "thorny" problem, so to speak. Plants respond to light and other physical stimuli; some plants are even reported to have a fairly developed nervous system. Where then do we draw the line? Can we say that all life is sacred without contradicting ourselves in our disregard for plant life, insects, bacteria, etc.? And could we survive without the classifications which allow us to eat, use, and destroy some life forms? Clearly, the sanctity of life is a function of our intelligent ordering; it is something which is deemed sacred by someone. Likewise, evil and goodness are expressions of our favor and disfavor; they are our judgment about ourselves in relation to nature and vice versa. So the problem of evil is not simply a question of existence simpliciter, but a question of the interpretation of existence. Also, nature by itself (that is, without intelligent beings) has no evil or goodness in it. Nature's goodness and/or evil is intentional; it is good or evil *for someone*.

We return then to our original postulate that the concept of evil, in whatever context, turns on the axis of meaning. As such, evil is not a primary experience but the interpretation of such an experience. And because every interpretation carries with it an interpreter, it follows that subjectivity must be the locus for meaning.

Intelligent beings cannot but respond to the world with some sense of order. To this end, we tend to experience life as an organic unity.[20] This, in turn, naturally predisposes us to make affirmations and denials in keeping with the unity of which we are a part. With this in mind, we would like to propose that experience is built upon certain pillars of belief which include: (1) the intrinsic value of life, (2) growth and development, (3) the right to happiness, (4) the expectation that everything, more or less, fits together, and (5) the possibility of an enduring meaning and purpose of life. We might call these beliefs: sanctity, becoming, bliss, order, and immortality, respectively. All of these beliefs are reflected in our judgments—judgments which affirm or question the meaningfulness of life. But even when the meaning of life is questioned, it is done from the perspective of a meaning frame (which is threatened with incompletion). What is noteworthy, however, is that those elements of experience which seem to fit the above beliefs about life are deemed "good," while the contrary ones are called "evil." In others words, the ideas of completion, order, fulfillment and purpose are integral to the notion of goodness, while the opposites are seen as threats and therefore evil.

It is important to note that these "beliefs" about life are much more than assumptions—they function as *insights*, or what Husserl calls "seeing-intuition" (*Anschauungen*). One might even call them "empirical insights," in that they begin *in* and *with* experience. They do not arise in a vacuum, but from the correlation of the categorial and the sensuous elements of experience. We do not experience objects as mere particulars, but as combinations or networks. This implies order, completion and purpose, as well as invites value assessments. The subject is always connected to the order and purpose he sees and brings to experience. In other words, the subjective component of experience is indispensable; and as such every (subjective) act is value-laden. Thus, we experience things as "good" or "bad"; that is, as descriptions of our involvement with, and perspective on them. Hence every description of our awarenesses is a description of experience, and this satisfies the definition of an empirical description.

Furthermore, the patterns or principles we discover in experience are not simply plausible beliefs; they are the conditions for experience. Whether these patterns accurately describe (rather than prescribe) the limits of experience is always open to further investigation. However, patterns point to principles which, in turn, make the sensuous elements of experience intelligible. Experience is intelligible if it is coherent, and troubling if it is not. In the final analysis it must be acknowledged then that any intelligible account of experience has to begin with what holds together, rather than what does not; with what is known, rather than what is unknown; with what is orderly, rather than the disorderly. Based on the Judeo-Christian account, experience began when God created the universe *ex nihilo*; that is to say, when order began.

If evil is seen as the phenomenon of disorderliness we have to conclude that goodness (seen as order) is prior to evil in human consciousness. In other words, goodness is the synonym for intelligent order whereas evil is characterized as the frustration of order. It must be noted, however, that this distinction is somewhat different from Platonism, which characterizes evil as unreal. We are acknowledging that both good and evil are interpretations of experience, but that goodness is the description of the pattern against which evil is measured. In fact, it is not uncommon to hear someone speak of evil as "the falling apart of life." Yet, this judgment could not have been made without some sense of an underlying order, albeit temporarily lost.

George Hendry—*The Theology of Nature*—while noting the presence of evil in a world created by a good God says that:

> . . . one thing may be said: the disorder in the world, which is the cause of so much suffering, becomes problematical only because it stands out from the order, which is the cause of well-being. It is the pervasive presence of order in the structure and workings of the world that throws the fact of disorder into relief; it is the exception to the rule, if not the exception that proves the rule.[21]

This acknowledgment does not claim that the familiar is good while the unfamiliar is evil; neither does it mean that evil is always unexpected while goodness is to be expected. There are numerous instances of persons who are surprised by things they consider good, as well as by things they consider evil. In fact, intelligent order is the structure of subjective life, and any deviation therefrom which threatens this order also threatens subjectivity. Intelligence must therefore begin with, and in, order before it becomes aware of disorder or evil. Alternatively, we might say that intelligence is characterized by order even if it has to struggle through the labrynths of (apparent) disorder.

Concluding Observation

Our discussion thus far has established that order is a *given* in experience; it is a necessary condition for experiencing the world of things and values.   Thus, the order we bring to experience is the structure through which every phenomenon receives identity and relatedness.   Order is not only a fundamental given for intentionality, i.e., interpretation, but also for being. Our very identities arise in order and are brought to all of our experiences.   Where the order we are (being), and the (dis-)order we perceive (as non-being) are in conflict, then the threat of alienation arises.   The threat of alienation, internally or externally, is a threat to self; it is a threat to our *constituting* ability (interpretation) as well as to our *constituted* preunderstanding (*being*).

Secondly, where order is threatened (and correspondingly, identity), then it is natural to expect that defensive and/or offensive measures will be taken to protect and enlarge one's sense of order. We might add, therefore, that whereas the notion of order can sometimes function as a metaphysical category, the protection of order is axiological.   In other words, defensive and offensive measures are the concerns of morality, not metaphysics. Morality is not a joyous exclamation of goodness, but a cautious streamlining thereof. Thus, the values we ascribe to "what is" are sometimes nothing more than a response to "what might be otherwise."   That is, the value we ascribe to the order we are (identity), and the order by which we live (our "web of connectedness"), can become the basic motivation for morality. Richard Taylor is therefore correct in his assessment about good and evil. He writes:

> When obstacles and threats to a man's activity are encountered, he deems them bad, and when things that assist in his goal-seeking are discovered, he deems them good. . . . And it is just in the light of this fact that men draw the distinction between good and evil in the first place. A man regards those things as good which satisfy his conative nature, and bad, those that frustrate it.[22]

Thirdly, whereas metaphysics purports to encompass what is and what is not real, morality distinguishes between them by attaching values to each. It thereafter prescribes limits of understanding and behavior. Morality thereby becomes another way of achieving intelligent order (in addition to the basic structure of intentional consciousness); it is our way of regulating and enlarging "the given" order we find in and about us. As such, morality both preserves and extends the borders of those experiences we consider "wholesome." Thus, morality seeks unity by distinguishing between those acts which contribute to "the greatest good," and those which militate against it. In other words, morality is determined by the prior assessment of what is good and what is evil. And as we have established, that which is deemed good is that which is believed to underpin intelligent order—the order we are and live by; while that which is deemed evil is that which threatens this order.

Fourthly, it is from the threat of the order we are and live by that the matter of fear arises. Fear is not a response to evil, but a first step in the discrimination of what is pleasing (orderly), and what is not pleasing (dis-orderly). Thus, fear is a primary awareness of threatened order as well as the occasion for morality. In fact, theology and morality are both responses to threatened order. However, theology operates with a slightly different grammar than does morality.

Theology emphasizes evil and goodness as competing orders and attaches symbolic force to each. However, it is not always clear whether evil is the source of fear and goodness the source of confidence since the theological "symbols" of god and the devil carry such awesome power.[23] Within these competing orders stands frail humanity, threatened by the wiles of the devil and the jealousy of the divine. To follow the divine is to make many sacrifices and suffer many hardships—ostensibly for the greater good; while to follow the devil is selfishly to enjoy temporary pleasures without ultimate security. Both of these options generate fear; the one is heralded as the beginning of wisdom (Proverbs 1:7), while the other is reported to be the route to destruction.

Finally, there are those who have decided to take a secular route, rather than a theological one, using science, common sense pragmatism, and a new morality as their guides. Their basic axiom is that nature is orderly and beautiful, and that reason (*not faith*) is the tool to understand and regulate nature. Of course, among these are those who are intellectually less sophisticated but who, nevertheless, embrace the pragmatic approach to life. In any case, all of these persons must develop an interpretation of nature which accounts for the destabilizing forces in life.

The emphasis on the order and beauty of nature first gained ascendancy during the Enlightenment. The principal explanatory tool was Newtonian physics. George Hendry sums up this period well in the following quotation:

> Nature had been annexed by science, and it proved much more responsive to scientific investigation than to theological interpretation; the heavens no longer declared the glory of God, but the laws of Newton, and even the light, which had been ascribed to the first act of creation, had had to wait for him, as Pope suggested in his famous couplet
>
>> "Nature and Nature's laws lay hid in night;
>> God said, let Newton be! and all was light."[24]

However, Ernest Becker points out that the challenge of this new awareness of nature had a double edge: it was a challenge to the (prevailing) theological world-view, as well as a challenge to the putative orderliness of nature and reason. Therefore, man needed a new explanation which went beyond Newtonian optimism. According to this argument it seems that:

> If the new nature was so regular and beautiful, then why was there evil in the human world? Man needed a new theodicy, but this time he could not put the burden on God. Something entirely different had to be done to explain evil in the world, a theodicy without divine intervention. The new theodicy had to be a natural one, a "secular" one.[25]

Becker further notes that with the absence of God no comprehensive theodicy could be advanced.

> There could be no sensible explanation for all the
> evil to which life is subject, apart from a belief in
> God—certainly no explanation that mere mortals
> could attain. Consequently, man had to settle for a
> new *limited* explanation, an anthropodicy which
> would cover only *those evils that allow for human
> remedy.* The only way to achieve this new
> explanation was gradually to shift the burden from
> reliance on God's will to the belief in man's
> understanding and powers.[26]

Nevertheless, there are those who seem to be able to bracket out God—at least the prevailing notions about God—while seeking an answer to the many complexities of life. In many ways this is truly phenomenological; it is a struggle to understand the phenomena of experience without the theoretical blinders which guide, but limit "clear seeing." However, in spite of this "natural" approach, there is something in human nature which leads our thinking back to the notion of the divine. Whether we have a fairly developed theology, or a guarded agnosticism, we all tend to have, in some degree, what Gordon Allport calls a religious sentiment:

> It is the portion of personality that arises at the core
> of the life and is directed toward the infinite. It is
> the region of mental life that has the longest-range
> intentions, and for this reason is capable of
> conferring marked integration upon personality,
> engendering meaning and peace in the face of the
> tragedy and confusion of life.[27]

With this in mind, we can safely conclude that the problem of evil occasions the beginning of a religious understanding of life. In fact, in many religious communities, the awareness of the existence of evil is one of the preconditions for a *higher* understanding of life.

In our next and final chapter, we will (1) investigate the relationship between fear and evil based on the account of their origin in the book of Genesis; (2) try to establish whether evil has a peculiar religious grammar; (3) assess the value of faith and reason as they relate to evil; and (4) suggest a new focus for the discussion of the problem of evil.

NOTES

1. We have chosen to introduce the problem of evil, not as an isolated phenomenon but as a wider *context* (matrix) of life's troubling experiences. It is from the general context that we hope to arrive at a phenomenological hermeneutic of the many ways of interpreting anything as evil.

2. To claim that there might be phenomena existing outside of consciousness is to suggest two orders of existence and knowing, and thereby to rob the term existence of its significance. For in spite of Kant's epistemology (in terms of phenomena and noumena), existence does have a predicative force. If not, we would contradict ourselves by postulating non-existing phenomena. However, when existence takes on an act-quality (without disregarding its object-quality) we will discover that there are many ways to exist or have objects—by imagination, feelings, perceptions, seeing, etc. Thus, existence *simpliciter* is never an experience for conscious beings, because even when we contemplate its possibility we are thereby giving it significance. Therefore, existence has no significance outside of conscious life, and neither does evil.

3. Peter R. Baelz, *Christian Theology and Metaphysics* (Philadelphia: Fortress Press, 1968), p. 78.

4. Richard Taylor, *Good and Evil: A New Direction* (New York: Prometheus Books, 1984), p. 123.

5. Taylor speaks of conative beings as (sentient) ones with desires and goals, and agrees that they need not be intelligent (p. 124). We are arguing, however, that every desire is goal-directed, and, as such, it is a form of intelligent ordering, albeit in a rudimentary way.

6. With respect to the role that evil plays in African religion, Gwinyai H. Muzorewa writes: "Unlike western theology and philosophy, which spend much time trying to establish the origin of evil African traditional religion spends much time dealing with the causes and effects of evil..." An African theology that develops with this background may take the form of a problem-oriented theology (The Origins and Development of African Theology [Maryknoll, New York: Orbis Books, 1985], p. 15).

7. Ibid., p. 12.

8. Gleaned from Fredrik Lindström, *God and the Origin of Evil* (Liberforlag Lund, Sweden: CWK Gleerup, 1983), p. 12, where the idea of a God of goodness and evil is discussed. It is important to note here also that Isaiah 45:7 records a stunning claim of YHWH: "I make peace, and create evil" (KJV).

9. Richard Rubenstein, *After Auschwitz* (New York: The Bobbs-Merrill Company, 1966), p. 153.

10. Hume, David. *Dialogues Concerning Natural Religion.* Edited with an Introduction by Norman Kemp Smith

(Indianapolis: Bobbs-Merrill Press, 1980), p. 66.

11.   Admittedly, this is a rationalistic assessment of morality—one which treats good and evil, and right and wrong as realities beyond (or in spite of) human will. One finds this approach to morality from Plato to the Enlightenment, with scattered pockets of support in Modern and Contemporary moral philosophy.

12.   For an engaging and informative discussion of the moral and theological significance of Plato's *Euthyphro*, please see A. E. Taylor, *Plato: The Man and His Work* (New York: The Dial Press, 1936), pp. 146-56. The reader will also find a sympathetic understanding of Euthyphro's position (over against Socrates') in Paul Friedlander, *Plato* (New York: Bollingen Foundation/Random House, 1964). A more recent discussion is Hanink & Mag, "What Euthyphro Couldn't Have Said" in *Faith and Philosophy* Vol. 4, No. 3, pp. 241-261.

13.   Richard Taylor, *Good and Evil*, pp. 126-27.

14.   Ibid., pp. 126-127.

15.   We will be arguing in the final section that whereas goodness (in the form of order) is a metaphysical given, evil is the occasion for morality. That is, evil gives rise to the need for rules of conduct by which it can be curtailed or minimized. As will be seen, this is a slightly different argument than the one presented by Richard Taylor.

16. Every phenomenon of thought, action, or material existence is natural. However, the term nature, as it is used in ordinary parlance, is attenuated to mean those things or occurrences which take place (or exist) in spite of human will. By this understanding, nature pre-dates our judgments about it. But is there not a place in "the natural realm" for human consciousness? The answer is quite "naturally" in the affirmative if the locution and the reality ("nature") is to have any meaning at all.

17. Kohák, *Idea and Experience*, p. 79.

18. Ibid., p. 78.

19. However, it does seem that the concept of evil carries more freight than simply a critique of existence (seen as a cosmological flaw). The extent of this alleged flaw is what human intelligence seeks to understand and remedy. But it could also be that the putative flaw grows exponentially in relation to the pursuit of its origin, and in this regard, the search is quixotic. This is, in essence, what the existentialists call the absurdity of existence.

20. Robert Nozick, *Philosophical Explanations* (Cambridge, Mass.: The Belknap Press of Harvard University, 1981), speaks of the organic unity which is presupposed in, and accompanies all our judgments. See pp. 415-50.

21. George Hendry, *The Theology of Nature* (Philadelphia: The Westminster Press, 1980), p. 183.

22.   Richard Taylor, *Good and Evil*, p. 147.

23.   Some will quickly demur that God is not a symbol of goodness but that he/she is the source of all that is good. However, we are defining symbol here as that which stands within human experience and yet not entirely explained by it. In short, the symbol of the divine explains human existence.

24.   Hendry, *The Theology of Nature*, p. 14.

25.   Ernest Becker, *The Structure of Evil* (New York: The Free Press, 1968), p. 18.

26.   Ibid.

27.   Gordon W. Allport, *The Individual and His Religion* (New York: The MacMillan Company, 1970), p. 161.

CHAPTER VI

FEAR AND THE LANGUAGE OF EVIL

We began this study with the bold claims that fear is more primary than evil; that it is an interpreting experience, whereas evil is the interpretation given to some experiences; that fear arises within the vortex of certain fundamental ambiguities; and that the grammar of fear can serve as a propaedeutic to the study of the problem of evil. These matters and more, have been addressed in the preceding chapters, but we have yet to establish the link between fear and evil.

In Chapter V we noted that fear is the first step in the discrimination of what is pleasing and displeasing, and thereby what is believed to be orderly and disorderly. We emphasized that fear is not a detached interpretation of phenomena but an *involved* relationship (of threat) therewith. As such, fear implies a threat to identity (being) as well as to the relationships (interpretations) by which identity is characterized. Fear is involved in the fundamental expressions of identity-relations. As an interpreting experience, it brings together both being and interpretation (object and subject) in a critical mode of consciousness which goes beyond intentionality. It is in this sense that we continue to maintain that fear is a *radical* catalyst for understanding; it is the expression of a critical consciousness which gives momentum to the dialectical process. And it is important to note that the dialectic of fear is not simply a *grasping* of objects, but a grasping of objects *as if* . . . In others words, fear puts experience in a subjunctive mood from which it derives the discriminating imperatives of identity and alienation, power and powerlessness, life and death (being and non-being).

What needs to be addressed in this section then is the

crucial link between fear and evil—the link which must be established if our thesis is to stand.

In order to establish this connection we need to be clear about our use of the term "evil." The "contexts" we enunciated in Chapter V are instructive here, but we want to go beyond that comparative approach and declare that the concept of evil has its roots in the religious forms of life. So although the locution "evil" has a secular currency, we are maintaining that it is its religious "reserves" which finally determine its rate of exchange. As Wittgenstein states it: ". . . to imagine a language means to imagine a form of life."[1] In other words, the language game of evil carries with it a religious way of interpreting experience. And whether we are talking about the dualism of ancient Zoroastrianism, the karma of Hinduism, the nirvana of Buddhism, the fatalism of Islam, or the frustrating ambiguities of the Judeo-Christian faith, evil functions as a central notion in religion. However, it is to the Judeo-Christian understanding of evil that we shall turn for our clue to the connection between fear and evil.

A. Fear and Evil

In his insightful little book on the problem of evil, Harold S. Kushner presents a provocative interpretation of the "forbidden" Tree (of the knowledge of good and evil) of which the book of Genesis speaks. He points out that this Tree is distinguishable from the Tree of Life: the one is for intelligent beings, while the other is for beings who operate at the level of instinct. He expresses the distinction thus: "Like our almost-but-not-quite-human ancestors, animals eat from the Tree of Life; they eat and drink, they run and they mate. But the Tree of Knowledge of

Good and Evil is off limits to them."[2]

Kushner is here distinguishing between two forms of goodness: that which is blissful and identical with life, and that which is rational and responsible (moral), and is thereby an extension of life. By this interpretation, our almost-human ancestors enjoyed a kind of metaphysical goodness (order), but the knowledge of good and evil is reserved for intelligent beings, who alone are capable of morality. By implication, morality replaces metaphysics as a means of personal and communal wholeness in intelligent communities. But morality is not only a new way of organizing phenomena, it is also a self-conscious (intelligent) description of the "limits" of existence. It is an effective way of dealing with the threat of *disorderliness*—a way of putting things back together, albeit, imperfectly. And in the final analysis, all self-conscious beings must experience the brokenness of existence and struggle to find worthwhile syntheses.

John Macquarrie believes that the brokenness of existence is brought home to consciousness via "limit-situations" which also serve as occasions for self-understanding. He says that

> . . . . finitude and fragmentariness are the essence
> of man's being. But ordinarily they escape notice
> or lie beneath the surface of our everyday
> awareness, so that it is only in something like a
> "limit-situation" that they come explicitly before us
> and we become a question to ourselves. . . .
> Actually . . . the limit-situation remains the place
> where the essential structures of our everyday living
> are lit up for us.[3]

Macquarrie's insights are useful here; they imply that rational existence reveals the brokenness of existence as well as occasions it, such that *the seeing becomes the seen.* In other words, the limit-situations, through which fragmentation become known, are themselves the products of self-consciousness. Outside of self-consciousness everything is an undifferentiated unity, and *questions* do not arise at this level. This is essentially what Kushner means by the "almost-human" existence of our ancestors—an existence without conscious distinctions.

Furthermore, the limit-situations function as catalysts for understanding, inasmuch as they confront us with the threats of alienation, powerlessness, and non-being. We characterize these situations as the marks of finitude. But this characterization does not fully explain the threats; it simply puts a tentative handle on these disquieting conditions. In point of fact, fear is the act through which we become aware of limit-situations, as well as the motivation to "handle" them. In this regard, fear becomes a tool for understanding, although *not all understanding is advanced by fear.* In a very loose sense, *healthy fear* is the beginning of wisdom.

Putting tentative handles on phenomena is a fundamental part of the process of understanding; yet, these so-called "handles" are not to be confused with understanding as such. There are many approaches to the understanding of disquietude, and fear is an important element of each.[4] Fear is a mode of self-consciousness which reveals one's vulnerability. However, as a motivation for understanding, fear also occasions ways of addressing the threats of brokenness experienced through self-conscious awareness. We see this "piecing together" of broken existence, in the story of Adam and Eve, as a function of morality.

The biblical account of how evil entered human experience emphasizes the *nakedness* (vulnerability) of self-consciousness. It shows, on the one hand, man's will to become, and on the other hand, man's unpreparedness for becoming. The former is dramatized as reflective curiosity, and the latter as natural inability.

As the story goes, the serpent reasons with Eve that God forbids their eating from the tree of good and evil simply because He wants to keep them in ignorance. In other words, to have a handle on goodness one must be able to distinguish good from evil.

> So when the woman saw that the tree was good for food, and that it was a delight to the eyes, and that the tree was to be desired to make one wise, she took of its fruit and ate; and she also gave some to her husband, and he ate. Then the eyes of both were opened, and they knew that they were naked; and they sewed fig leaves together and made themselves aprons.[5]

There are several things worth noting in this account, among which are: (1) the subtlety of the serpent; (2) Eve's susceptibility to natural subtleties; (3) her interest in extending her consciousness beyond the "givens" to the "discoverables" in creation, in contradistinction to Adam's apparent diffidence; (4) her willingness to gain knowledge by reason/experience rather than by mere faith; and (5) the self-critical posture (nakedness) which results from the knowledge of good and evil. All of these points converge on the notion of the *painful* responsibilities of self-discovery. And it is precisely at the point of the *threatening awareness of pain* that the locution "evil"—the knowledge of good and evil—gains significance.

In order to have the knowledge of good and evil one has to

be self-conscious. That is, one has to be able to distinguish oneself from everything else while holding on to everything. This is a classic case of eating one's cake while having it—a function of God, not men, as the Genesis account makes known. But whether or not the divine is successful at this feat is not the point. What is noteworthy is that when humans attempt self-discovery something "old" has to be sacrificed for something "new." Discovery involves a new way of seeing; it is a discriminatory view rather than a collective view. In the case of Adam and Eve it is also a personal and goal-directed view (i.e., comprehensive knowledge), rather than an other-directed view. Every such view carries certain responsibilities; one gives up the security of Eden when one ventures beyond its limits. Being aware of the world as an undifferentiated unity (of which we are a part) is quite different from seeing the world from the perspective of *willful* distinctions; that is, from the perspective of good and evil. The one pictures everything *in place*, while the other shows disunities, discords, and naked separations. This is the burden of responsibility associated with self-conscious will. Self-consciousness promises pleasure, freedom and confidence, but these are bought at the price of pain, new limits, and the threat of naked separation.

Thus, in keeping with our argument in Chapter II, we want to state that fear arises when we discover that our identity, and the power to protect it, is threatened. The account of Adam and Eve indicated that evil arose when they opened themselves to a *different* hermeneutic of order and goodness. The metaphorical serpent introduced a competing order of life which, when accepted, disrobed Adam and Eve of their protective identity-garment of goodness. The removal of this protection occasions fear, or more apt, knowledge *with* and *through* fear.

The serpent succeeded in distinguishing **order** from **value** and **being** from **interpretation**, and thereby introduced a fearsome separation into the consciousness of Adam and Eve. To wit, the hermeneutic of the serpent suggests that goodness is not something which is given, but discovered; it is not merely theological, but rational/experiential. In other words, goodness is not a divine token but a human challenge and, as such, it is an expression of knowledge rather than an extension of being. Besides, the comprehensive reach of knowledge (which the subtle reason of the serpent promises) is most attractive. After all, if God has this comprehensive knowledge it cannot be all bad; at least, this seems to have been Eve's response. For as long as the knowledge is not of *evil alone*, but of good and evil, there is no real reason not to seek it.[6]

However, in spite of the plausible argument of the serpent its hermeneutic is theologically inverted. It explicitly rejects the notion that "what ought to be" is "what is." It states, contrary to God's command, that "you will not die" (Genesis 3:4) if you eat the fruit of the tree of good and evil. In addition, its hermeneutic implicitly denies that "what is" is "what ought to be"; that is, the serpent claims that knowledge is a function of inquiry and experience, not of fiats. Thus, the serpent was intent on destablizing (and changing) the order and nature of things in the Garden. The extent of the serpent's subtlety is the valueless universe into which it tricked Adam and Eve. This valueless and unprotective universe forcibly opened their eyes to a naked existence. This is the nadir of metaphysical and moral nihilism; a state of affairs in which one is unprotected, and vulnerable, and where one *passes one's life* in "the valley of the shadow of death" rather than live under the shade of the tree of life. This is a cringing form of existence rather than a lively and buoyant one. Thus, as God approached, Adam hid himself and later states: "I heard you in the garden, and I was *afraid* because I was naked; so I hid."[7] [Emphasis mine.]

Although guilt and shame are obviously involved in this episode, it is interesting that fear is emphasized as the medium through which Adam and Eve became conscious of their separation from the divine. Their fear was not simply a fear of God, but also the fear of facing God in separation from him; that is, facing God as a "Wholly-Other," to borrow Rudolf Otto's famous term. According to Otto, "the 'wholly other' . . . is quite beyond the sphere of the usual, the intelligible, and the familiar. . . ."[8] In other words, there is a feeling of an overpowering mystery associated with the presence of the divine once one is separated from the divine's nurturing and enfolding embrace.

What Adam and Eve discovered then was the sense of inadequacy attendant to the act of trying to approximate the mystery of divine knowledge, the concomitant feelings of separation and abasement, and the awfulness of facing God as Judge rather than as Protector (Advocate). They sought knowledge beyond the borders of order and goodness; interpretation beyond the given; and unity beyond the whole. In the process they lost what they had before, as well as failed to integrate that which they found—the knowledge of good and evil. They lost their protection, their identity, and their unity with God and nature. As a result, they tried in vain to fabricate their own protection against disorder and meaninglessness. But there were no natural substitutes for divine protection, because nature itself seems to be responsive to divine will. Consequently, if divine protection is expressed through nature, and man is out of step with the divine, then nature will be unresponsive to man. It is little wonder then that God says that the ground will become a curse to man in his state of estrangement:

> . . . . cursed is the ground because of you; in toil you shall eat of it all the days of your life; thorns and thistles it shall bring forth to you. . . . . In the sweat of your face you shall get bread till you return to the ground. . . .[9]

This pronouncement seems to be the blue-print for a remedial program to assist mankind in the recovery of some modicum of order. It serves as a punishment for disobedience, as well as a preparation for responsibility. It is a judicial sentence to hard labor (Genesis 3:19) with a set of guiding principles. And since Adam and Eve were no longer protected by an orderly (unitary) goodness, they now had to struggle to regain order and goodness through morality and labor.[10]

This account shows that with man's alienation from God comes also his alienation from material creation (as well as from himself and others): "Man's work now comes under a curse."[11] However, James Plastaras states that "it is man alone who has changed,"[12] not God or nature. But when man changes he undoubtedly becomes self-conscious and sees everything from the perspective of threat. On this point Plastaras emphatically asserts:

> Certainly God had not changed, but man, because of the change which had taken place within him, had remade God into another image and likeness. From now on the characteristic attitude of man in the presence of the divine would tend to be fear. . . . In this state of alienation, man would see God

even as a hostile threatening force.. . .[13]

It would appear that our personalities develop a critical edge when our experiences become confrontational, combative, and seemingly capricious. In this state, work becomes drudgery, things become obstacles, people become competitors, and life becomes threateningly difficult. Praise and blame now become the distinguishing measures of our comforts and discomforts. Those things which threaten us receive blame, and those that undergird us receive praise. When we translate the language of praise and blame, in the case of Adam and Eve, we arrive at "the knowledge of good and evil." One simply needs to look at the litany of blame which each gave to God, in support of this thesis. Thus, the symbol of the knowledge of good and evil finds expression in praise and blame: "The symbol reveals experience through expression; the myth interprets the expression which the symbol gives,"[14] according to Don Ihde.

Fear and evil coalesce at the level of experience and interpretation, or symbol and expression. The experience of separation inevitably leads to a state of vulnerability. Feelings of acute separation tend to give the rest of life a symbolic power which, in turn, activates and potentiates our fears. We speak of "the crushing weight of responsibilities" when we have no real support from others; "the coldness of a new community," when we are unable to make connections; and "the overpowering void" in one's life, after the death of a loved one. In other words, the object of fear becomes an evil when it separates us from order (and goodness). Thus, to know evil is to know separation, and the experience of separation makes us see order *from the outside*—beyond the limits of goodness. In the experience of separation, disorder is always presented against the order we know; it is an exile experience of sorts. But it is important to note that the very threat of such an experience is enough to make one troubled.

Notwithstanding, John Macquarrie claims that the anxieties of separation not only make us acutely aware of limit-situations, but of possible ways of dealing with finite existence: ". . . the very attainment of such an awareness is also a transcending of mere transience, and is the awakening of the quest for grace and meaning. This is the starting point for religious language, and, *a fortiori*, for theological language."[15] Thus fear can give rise to both the acknowledgment of evil and the acceptance of a new order (even grace). In this latter case, fear is the beginning of understanding, if not wisdom.

B. Evil and Religious Language

Religious language consists of three principal elements, all of which must be acknowledged in an understanding thereof. First, there are the language users, which we will call "the community of users"; then there are the objects of use, which we will call "religious objects"; and, finally, there are the attitudes of the users toward the objects, which we will call "the religious attitude." This *formal* description of religious language accentuates the fact that language does not arise in a vacuum, or outside of a community, but that it is the fabric in which a way of life is woven. Thus, to understand the *material* expressions (contents) of any religious community, one has to pay attention to the function (and grammar) these expressions have in the life of the community. This involves, as a primary task, the understanding of the community.

On the other hand, there are material contents which are shared by different communities of users, as well as contents which seem to stand in conflict. In fact, there is so much diversity of users and attitudes that it is often quite difficult definitively to identify what counts or does not count as a religious object. It is for this reason that we have restricted our focus to the religious language of the Judeo-Christian tradition. Having done so, we are thereby dealing with a segment of religious language, namely, Judeo-Christian theological statements.

According to John Macquarrie, theological language arises out of religious language as a whole, and it does so when a religious faith becomes reflective and tries to give an account of itself in verbal statements. This does not mean, however, that worship and ritual are unimportant; rather, these forms of religious behavior are given verbal expression: "What is done (ritual) perhaps came before what is said (myth), but the myth and the ritual go together in a reciprocal interpretation of each other . . ." Thus, religious language does not consist of *simple beliefs*; that is, beliefs functioning as hypotheses, but of *a way of life*. Macquarrie puts the entire matter in perspective when he states that:

> Theology itself lives and has its meaning only in relation to the wider matrix from which it arises. When it strays too far from its source or when it gets separated from other modes of expression in worship and ethics, it degenerates into empty and arid disputes; and of course, if it has become detached from its living background and then gets subjected in an artificial way to some formal analysis, we must not be surprised if it begins to appear senseless.[16]

Macquarrie's understanding of religious language (and its theological expressions) coheres with our declared Wittgensteinian methodology. In an exposition of Wittgenstein's influence on religious discourse Alan Keightley remarks that "Theology gives *expression* to a particular way of life. Words alone are empty of life. They have to be nourished by their use in a community."[17] It is this awareness that we propose to pursue in the matter of evil. That is, we will investigate the use of the term evil to see whether it belongs exclusively to a religious form of life.

If it is true that religious language reflects a "form of life" and that all "forms of life" have their own peculiar grammar and "language-games," then what is the status of the word "evil?"

Religious language does not necessarily consist of different words, or even expressions, from the general language (say, of French or English) in which it is expressed. Its difference is one of *emphasis* and *significance*. For example, a "cross" is an identifiable object in most languages, but its significance for Christians goes beyond a mere thing-identification to a symbolic entity. Symbols, unlike mere objects, are not simply things to be interpreted, but things through and by which we interpret. Thus a symbol is not an ostensive tool but an intentional medium; it facilitates analogy by reaching beyond itself. A cross is not only a vertical pole with a horizontal bar, but a symbol of Christian courage and hope. To remove the cross from its Christian context is to rob it of its rich symbolism, or to give it new significance.

We are claiming then that religious language is metaphorical; it includes rituals, symbols and myths, among other features. But the peculiar feature of this language is that it has *an ordinary locus with an extra-ordinary focus*. As theology, it has a grammar which "articulates the standards of intelligibility implicit in the language and activities of a religious tradition." Part of the grammar of religious tradition is "faith, and love"; the basic principles by which the community of users are organized. Of course, the central object of theological language is God; he/she who is the source of all understanding, all hope and all life. Macquarrie puts it well when he declares that theology is God-talk: "the whole theological vocabulary is tied in with the word 'God.' It is this word that . . . organizes or coordinates the others within a framework of significance."[18] Faith is the religious attitude of the community of users, hope is its expectation and commitment to renewal, and love its source and consuming passion. All of these expressions are directed to God, as well as to the understanding of what pleases God (love of neighbor, self and ecological responsibility). However, it is its peculiarly strong emphasis on the future (which God controls) that distinguishes theological language from ordinary discourse.

Theological language is *teleological*, or more to the point, *eschatological*. It sees the present in the light of the future, and the future in the present. Its universe of discourse is very open, albeit with a restricted focus. Yet, it is not unaware of those experiences which cast a shadow over the future; experiences which suggest that there is no purpose, or that God is not in control. These experiences cannot be the rule of order and goodness, but must necessarily belong to the disorderly rule of evil. The experiences which are interpreted as evil are those which suggest that the future is not in God's hands. That is, those experiences which suggest that the system of intelligibility (order) associated with divine administration is suspended. This is equivalent to a *coup d'etat* (rebellion) against God; a state of affairs in which the borders of orderly expectations are closed, orderly relations are breached, benevolent protection has ceased, and indecency released. And experience has taught us that one coup leads to another, or as the Bible puts it, the sins of the parents extend to the third and fourth generations of those who do not fear the Lord.[19] That is, those who do not look to the Lord as their only source of order and interpretation will become part of the continuing rebellion against him.

Once there is a successful rebellion against God the ripple effects will be felt for all times. To paraphrase I Corinthians 15:22a: "In Adam all have sinned." In other words, part of the inverted purpose of evil is to cast doubt on God's ability to maintain orderly control. It only takes one example of successful rebellion to fill us with dis-ease. Theological language seeks to rise above this gnawing doubt (about God's nature and purpose) without losing sight of it. In the terminology of Paul Ricoeur, theological language constitutes a *hermeneutic of faith* and a *hermeneutic of suspicion*—two opposing hermeneutics which must be dialectically synthesized if theology is to maintain coherence. For while the task of faith is the nurture of meaning, as well as the restoration of lost meaning, the task of suspicion is quite different. As Ricoeur says:

> I call suspicion the act of dispute exactly proportional to the expressions of false-consciousness. The problem of false-consciousness is the object, the correlative of the act of suspicion. Out of it is born the quality of doubt, a type of doubt which is totally new and different from Cartesian doubt.[20]

In other words, suspicion is a form of demystification which seeks to *destroy* some forms of traditional meaning. And as Ricoeur goes on to say "there is a profound unity between *destroying* and *interpreting,"* and that "any modern hermeneutics is a hermeneutics with a double edge and a double function."

Alternatively, we might say that whereas *fear* is a critical consciousness of disorder (evil), *faith* is an affirming consciousness of the final resolution of disorder. Stated thus, the grammar of fear becomes a disquieting expectation, and the grammar of faith becomes eschatological. Fear is thereby the awareness which leads to both suspicion and faith, destruction and interpretation, the knowledge of good and evil. The object of fear is here opposed to the object of hope, but it is the task of theology to show how the latter object can transform fear into faith (i.e., from an awareness of disorder to a *commitment* to order). In which case fear will be more than courage, it will truly become the beginning of wisdom.

Religious language is therefore the language-game most appropriate to the term evil. It interprets the composite of disorderliness which seeks to frustrate God's plan for the human community as evil. Every violation of divine order is thereby a challenge to God. This is why the symbolic force of evil involves much more than "things going wrong;" it also implies an attack on God's goodness, order, purpose, power and omniscience. That things go wrong would not constitute evil necessarily, but that things go wrong because of a contrary will (internally and externally), suggests that God is being challenged. This is the force of the serpent's subtle reason: "you will not surely die." Or in the words of the ungodly: "How can God know? Does the Most High have knowledge?" (Psalm 73:11—NIV). Some even deny the existence of God and thereby claim that Her putative order is an illusion. The psalmist calls these persons fools,[21] (notwithstanding Ricoeur's acknowledgment of the rich hermeneutical possibilities of Marx, Nietzsche and Freud). It is clear, however, that the Bible spurns the foolishness of those who would seek knowledge—even the knowledge of good and evil— without the fear of the Lord. The foolish person is he who replaces fear with reason, whereas the wise person is he who replaces it with faith. The one naturalizes and demystifies the idea of evil, whereas the other offers "the sacrifice of a broken heart" in the hope of renewal (Psalm 51:17).

But is the matter as simple as this? Does not religious language employ the tenets of "sound" reason in the articulation of its percepts? Isn't it quite clear that no system of belief could survive without some rationale for its being? The articulation of the *raison d'etre* of any faith is what helps it to win converts as well as form the core of its language-games. That its grammar is different does not mean that it is void of reason (in its most general sense), as we shall see below.

C. Reason, Faith and Evil

We want to acknowledge that religious language, inasmuch as a language is a coherent system for communication, is "rational." This means that religious language has a basis for beliefs as well as procedures for justifying these beliefs. Whether its method of justification is adequate is a matter to be determined by the context of the specific claims being made. Secondly, it must be stressed that where religious claims purport to deal with "non-religious objects" without acknowledging the contexts of these objects, then it is guilty of what Gilbert Ryle calls a category mistake.

Thirdly, analytic philosophers have noted that religious

statements tend to claim all possible states of affairs and thereby trivialize the notion of proof. As Frederick Ferré notes: "When *any* state of events is compatible with an assertion, then the putative assertion is either analytic or meaningless." This is a reasonable analysis, it seems; for if God answers prayers—and prayers are partly for specific things—then there should be some means of verifying whether or not specific prayers are answered. But when we claim that God answers prayers, while praying for specific things, and then conclude that whatever results is God's answer, we have changed the interpretation of "answer," "results" and the terms of reason.

Frederick Ferré explains that

> Verificational analysis provides a logical account of why an explanation, if it is to explain, must explain *some* events and not others: if a theory is open to confirmation by any experience whatever, it is saying nothing in particular. But to say nothing in particular is equivalent to saying nothing at all! For this reason all explanations which are logically able to explain—able, that is, to have a definite factual meaning—must be of limited generality.[22]

Ferré acknowledges, however, that the theists are more interested in supernatural, rather than natural explanations. This is what we earlier called the extraordinary focus beyond an ordinary locus.

> Religious statements are of this type. They refer without exception to things that cannot be established as physical facts. If they did not do this, they would inevitably fall into the category of the natural sciences. Taken as referring to anything physical, they make no sense whatever, and science

would dismiss them as non-experienceable. They would be mere miracles, which are sufficiently exposed to doubt as it is, and yet they could not demonstrate the reality of the spirit of *meaning* that underlies them, because meaning is something that always demonstrates itself and is experienced on its own merits.[23]

Unlike the verificationists, Jung (in his *Answer to Job*) does not rule out the emotions as a medium of truth. He says that "'physical' is not the only criterion of truth: there are also *psychic* truths which can neither be explained nor proved nor contested in any physical way.[24] Religious language organizes facts in such a way that they add up to more than an aggregate of things; they fecundate an element of significance beyond the discernible totality of things. This, in itself, is an extension of meaning (beyond proof) to commitment. Thus, it is not just the facts which are organized but also the persons for and by whom they are organized. In this way, the rationality of religious meaning is found in its way of life—*Lebensform*. This bears some resemblance to what Ferré makes explicit in the words of John Wisdom. He says that: "The function of theological discourse . . . is to *direct our attention* to patterns in 'the facts.'"

But even though theological discourse is not open to the same rational procedures as the natural sciences, this does not mean that it has no justifying procedures. For as John Wisdom puts it, ". . . . we must not forthwith assume that there is no right and wrong about it, no rationality or irrationality, no appropriateness or inappropriateness, no procedure which tends to settle it, nor even that this procedure is in no sense a discovery of new facts."[25] Ferré quotes a constellation of philosophers who agree that theological discourse has unique functions which include worship (J. J. C. Smart, E. L. Allen), conviction (Willem Zuurdeeg), commitment via paradox (I. T. Ramsay), and illumination of one's understanding of the world (Ian Crombie).[26]

We acknowledged in the previous chapter that evil poses a challenge to intelligent existence because it frustrates order. This acknowledgment puts the question of evil on the level of the search for understanding. The two most familiar paths to the understanding of religious phenomena are faith and reason.

Evil is a problem for both faith and reason because, in different ways, it introduces the notion of incompletion. Specifically, evil is a problem for reason because it represents an objection to the ultimate coherence of the phenomena of experience. Nonetheless, the optimism of reason is that the universe is rational, and that, with time and intelligent effort, everything will eventually fall in place. Those phenomena which defy rational explanation can be bracketed either as irrational, or as criteriological "misfits." In this way, the putative problem of evil is "frozen" or explained away. But reason is not as attenuated and exclusive as some would like to define it. Reason is an activity of consciousness whereby order is drawn from, or imposed upon phenomena. Both the drawing and the imposing of phenomena can be explained in some way or other.

That some phenomena seem to stand outside of the range of reason is an indication that reason is not absolute rather than that the phenomena are unreal. Some of the experiences we call evil are of this type, and we are sometimes led to say that "there is *no reason* for these occurrences." Reason is therefore the term applied to the many ways of ordering phenomena; each way reflects a form of life for which reasons can be adduced. However, the peculiarity of the rational approach to order is that it deftly outlines limits of clarity which seek to avoid unnecessary ambiguity. Yet, the richness of experience and language lies in the ambiguous; and it is from this ambiguous, uncharted, terrain that "evil" arises as a challenge to reason. Is it any wonder then that evil is symbolized as "the dark region" of experience? After all, reason is acknowledged to be the secular symbol of light.

On the other hand, evil is a challenge to faith because it represents an objection to the belief in a comprehensive goodness (apotheosized as the divine). But whereas reason seeks to describe and explain the problem of evil, faith tends to symbolize evil. Thus, for faith evil is not simply a series of unfortunate occurrences, but a network of pestiferous and demonic acts. In either case, evil seems to symbolize reason's cul-de-sacs and faith's breaking points. Yet, it is precisely at these points that the test of reason's acuity and faith's importunacy can be demonstrated. In other words, evil represents the challenges to excellence and the frustration to faith and reason. It can either occasion the battle cry of the strong or the death cry of the weak and helpless.[27]

However, the theists do not think that we need to despair in helplessness, but that this very state can be the start of something *new* and promising, namely, faith. As the Psalmist puts it: "God is our refuge and strength, a very present help in trouble" (Psalm 46:1). Or in the oft quoted words of the writer of the Epistle to the Hebrews: "Faith is the substance of things hoped for, the evidence of things not seen" (Hebrews 11:1). Thus, faith is far more fundamental in dealing with the complexities of life than reason because it is intentionally related to a religious object (namely, God), whereas reason is not:

. . . . faith enables men to hope and believe there
is a genuine possibility of their reaching
responsibility   and freedom without destroying
themselves. Unfaith, however—believing man to be
fundamentally alone in the world as a purposive
being—can live with no such confidence and can
face the evils and difficulties of existence with no
such hopes.   For it knows of no cosmic
intentionality that wills man's existence and is
working for his successful emergence into full
humanity and humaneness.[28]

Faith is therefore connected to *something* in a way that
reason is not, and articulates more clearly the nature of human
experience (as intentional) than is otherwise believed. Kaufman
writes that

A man's resolve, therefore, to order his life
according to the demands of theistic faith (or
according to any other pattern, for that matter)
always remains a leap of faith, a willingness to
commit himself to a pattern of life as right and
good even though he is unable metaphysically or
logically to ground such a commitment.[29]

The theist's faith is in God, "the anchor-symbol for a whole
way of life and world view." This symbol "defines and orients a
whole way of life and understanding of the world,"[30] such that evil
is given a place. Thus, the existence of evil is not the crucial
problem for faith, but the possibility of existence without faith in
God. This is what gives force to theism's missionary zeal—the
conviction that evil can be overcome through faith in God.
"Believing in God thus means practically to order all of life and
experience in personalistic, purposive, moral terms, and to

construe the world and man accordingly. . . ."[31] Faith thereby becomes the motivation and tool for the understanding of life...the central move in the language-game of the theistic (Judeo-Christian) form of life.

But the theists need to distinguish more clearly between faith as a motivation for understanding (much in the terms of Augustine's and Anselm's *fides quarens intellectum*), and faith as a rationalization for misunderstanding. Here the philosopher John Hick is helpful, offering a distinction of faith *as interpretation*.

> Here "interpretation" does not mean intellectual interpretation or theory construction, but something more akin to the interpretative processes which take place in sense perception. From the point of view of epistemology, faith is thus analogous to the phenomenon of "seeing as," which was brought to the attention of philosophers by Ludwig Wittgenstein. . . .

What Hick is here addressing is the analogous seeing or experiencing which takes place in interpretation. That is, while nature forms the core of our experiences, its boundaries can be extended to include more than the factual contents of things.

> Indeed, it is always true of the religious mode of "experiencing as" that the data in question are in themselves ambiguous and capable of being responded to either religiously or naturalistically. More strictly, the two types of interpretation are not alternatives on the same level but are different orders of significance found in the same field of data.   The religious significance includes and transcends their natural significances.[32]   [Emphasis

mine.]

It is worth noting here that *faith as interpretation* is that which seeks understanding *within* and without nature. In point of fact, even though faith has its beginning within nature, its final destination is beyond nature. This is certainly more than a rationalization of misunderstanding or blind belief; it is a firm commitment to a way of life which *promises* goodness.

But can evil have any force against a faith that is "on its way to understanding?" Does not this "process" suggest that the problem of evil is at worst a challenge?

It is reasonable to argue that a faith which is on its way to (religious) understanding can experience no intractable problems, unless it is distracted by natural reason.[33] But this is not to suggest that faith can survive without reason. To put it another way, we do not only have to decide about what is a reasonable and what is a faithful response to experience, but also when it is reasonable to live *by faith alone*. The implication being that faith without the works of reason is blind belief, dogmatic rationalization, or simply posturing. Faith can no more function without reason than reason without faith. (Here "faith with reason," in contradistinction with "faith in reason," implies a firm belief in the adequacy of rational principles.)

In the final analysis, both reason and faith bring us face to face with limit-situations, and beyond the limits of knowledge and belief there is a peculiar chaos which repels and entices. To be enticed is to open oneself to the possibilities of the unknown, and this forces one to begin "from scratch." This is not only the founding principle of "phenomenological archeology," but the foundation of fear. (Kierkegaard even refers to life in this region as the beginning of faith.) The loss of assurance of benevolent limits (security) occasions an abysmal state of uncertainty which can only be called evil. However, even though reason spurns the abyss, faith enables one to walk through it without fear of evil (Psalm 23). But this is a radical faith which transcends the limits which fear makes known, and embraces the unexpected with a singular hope.

It is here that faith and reason *temporarily* part company, the point at which immediate awareness (consciousness) coalesces with being, and where the hoped for (the object) and the hoping (the act) are correlated in the hopeful (the subject). Here the faithful subject does not fear extinction since God is the source of being, as well as the effective advocate against non-being. Notwithstanding, it is the faithful subject's act (of faith) which brings him in touch with God or with self-understanding. In others words, all awarenesses can be reduced to acts of human consciousness, as Charles Courtney explains in the Introduction to Henry Duméry's *The Problem of God in Philosophy of Religion*:

> All significations, including the most abstract and
> general principles, are products of this act. Thus
> there is no way to God that leads directly from a
> system of ideas. The acting subject, rather than
> God, is at the end of any chain of ideas.[34]

This acting subject should be the focus for any study of the problem of evil.

D. A Phenomenology of Evil

To recommend that future studies of the problem of evil begin with the acting subject is not necessarily to introduce an anthropodicy. According to Frederick Sontag, anthropodicy means that we "no longer try to explain evil in the context of God but accept . . . that evil stems solely from the human conditions."[35] We are not saying that; rather, we are emphasizing that evil is a hermeneutical problem, and that all matters of interpretation begin with acting subjects (even if the interpretations end elsewhere). Moreover, attempting to *describe* the conditions of evil from the perspective of the acting subject is not antithetical to our acknowledgment that evil derives its symbolic force from a religious context. Sontag states this with unmistakable clarity when he says that: "The meaning of life is a religious problem and cannot be otherwise for us."[36] However, the central route to God is via human consciousness, as Charles Courtney reminds us above.

Secondly, our recommendation implicitly rejects the study of evil from the perspective of divine attributes. This traditional approach to the study of evil forces theism into logical contradiction: if God is *all* good, *all* wise, and *all* powerful, how can evil exist? In order to gain logical consistency the theist has to admit one of the following modifications: (1) that evil is unreal; (2) that God is benevolent but not omnipotent; (3) that God is omnipotent but not benevolent; or (4) that God is benevolent and omnipotent but not omniscient.

Experience refutes the first modification; besides, if there were not some disquieting experiences (evil) in the first instance, there would be no necessity for explanations. It is rather curious to explain *something* that is unreal. In fact, the whole problem of evil first arises as a question for human consciousness. Thus to say that evil is unreal is to cast doubts on the reliability of human consciousness and thereby plunge existence into a skeptical quagmire. And if evil did not exist before, this latter state of affairs would certainly bring it into existence.

The second modification admits that God is well-intentioned but lacks an effective will. This bears the image of a saintly, greying, lovable, though "toothless," grandfather who loves dearly, but who is not "nearly" as strong as his love. Likewise, the third modification makes God into a despot; he wields power in a capricious manner. While the fourth modification makes God into a bumbling, witless character who is as surprised and troubled by evil as are mere mortals.

None of these modifications is tenable, unless we are defining God from the perspective of evil, rather than evil from the perspective of the divine. The God of theism is *sui generis*; he/she is not an object (among others) to be explained, but that by which a theological explanation is possible. Failure to recognize this distinction results in the confusion of a defining principle with an instance of the principle itself.[37] In addition, these modifications do not only raise questions about God, but introduce difficulties of criteria and logic. For if logic is the tool by which criteria are judged then a God who is defined as absolute cannot be reduced to anything else without ceasing to be God. An attenuated concept of God, in contradistinction to an absolute, is one which denies what it wants to affirm; namely, divine supremacy.

In addition, it is questionable whether an absolutely good God could be powerless, or whether an absolutely good and powerful God could be unwise. For if goodness has any force, it cannot simply be well-intentioned, but also effective. This is the *Summum Bonum* of which Immanuel Kant speaks. Again, even if it were possible to be absolutely good but ineffective, one could not be absolutely powerful and good without the power of wisdom; if power is absolute it must also include wisdom. Thus the logical embarrassment of explaining evil from the perspective of divine attributes is a criteriological problem. That is, *the problem of evil has to be pursued from the perspective of what serves as a criterion of evil rather than what seeks to justify the existence of evil.* All justifications must be measured against the criteria they seek to express, and these criteria are more aptly *shown* in a form of life than *stated* in logical formulae.

For the theists, the problem of evil arises within the context of the inconsistencies of the divine attributes and the existential realities which these attributes should pre-empt. Logically stated, the problem of evil is a problem of God, but philosophically it is a problem of language. For although the problem of evil has to do with "the logic of expectation" (inference), it also requires a grammar of interpretation. Thus, in the final analysis, all theodicies and explanations are hermeneutical attempts in making experience's multivalency univocal, and experience's malevolencies benevolent. However, these require a carefully directed inquiry into the being of consciousness if coherence is to be attained.

Thirdly, we have emphasized throughout this investigation that a phenomenological study of consciousness (as act and object) is the most adequate route to the problem of evil. Our recommendation of the acting subject as the new focus for the study of the problem does not only seek to obviate unnecessary logical conundrums, but emphasizes the need for categorial origins. The former introduces the problem of evil as a problem of being without first attending to the meaning of being. But Charles Courtney, in his exposition of Duméry's philosophy of religion, states that:

> A philosophy that discovers consciousness to be the
> creator of all signification, including the meaning of
> being, is the only philosophy that can carry out a
> radical clarification of its foundations. In short, the
> advantage of a metaphysics of consciousness is that
> it can protect both its flanks; its starting point in
> pre-reflective consciousness is indubitable, and it
> can reveal the foundation of all its principles.[38]

This new starting point serves both as a *reduction* of the
symbolic (ontological) force of evil and of God. Reduction does
not seek out the object symbolized—God or evil—but the
conditions for their existence *as symbols*. Thus, if the symbol of
God gives rise to mysteries which are considered to be both good
and evil, then the reduction of this symbol should be illuminating;
it should reveal the conditions of the being of consciousness. In
other words, symbols are hermeneutical catalysts for
interpretation—they are not the repositories of meaning. It is for
this reason that God is not a mystery to himself, or evil an
independently existing phenomenon. The mystery of God is a
correlate of human consciousness, as is the presence of evil.

> . . . . God is not an ensemble of determinations
> beyond our grasp. The mystery comes from us
> who make the screen, not from God who is pure
> light. When we believe we unveil him, we veil
> him, since we compromise his unity. In this sense,
> God is the simple that we complicate, the One that
> we render "complex," the Absolute that we
> "relativize."[39]

Fourthly, and finally, a phenomenology of evil is a study of human consciousness in its *production* and *reduction* of objects. These objects have a religious form of life with a grammar which renders them coherent. The central object or symbol is God, but God is experienced in many ways; for example, in joys and sorrows. He is also a *given*, and as such, serves as a regulatory principle for experience and interpretation. Any attempt to redefine the principle by which one is regulated will result in confusion. For how can one successfully redefine his form of life without drawing on the same form of life in the redefinition? Or by what means can one get outside one's form of life other than by the form of life in question? This hermeneutical circle cannot be broken by any appeal to outside categories, but by a "perspicuous seeing." The issue therefore centers on human consciousness—the medium through which God is veiled and revealed. Wittgenstein puts it well when he says that: "You can't hear God speak to someone else, you can hear him only if you are being addressed.—That is a grammatical remark."[40]   Thus, if the understanding of evil is a function of the understanding of the divine, and the understanding of the divine a function of human consciousness, then the primary focus of the problem has to be human consciousness.

This involves, among other things, the two basic modes in which consciousness is exercised; namely, hope and fear. And as we have articulated before, our hopes are for identity, power, and a meaningful endurance through time, while our fears are the challenges to these; namely, alienation, powerlessness, and death. Finding the courage to synthesize dialectically our fears and hopes is the real challenge of consciousness; it calls for the radical transformation of fear into faith, and the extension of time into eternity. However, this is not done by shifting the focus from logic to theology, but by attending to the primary acts of consciousness.

Notwithstanding, within a religious form of life the primary determinant of meaning is God; God is that by which everything else gains significance. This does not only put God beyond question, but provides a way of seeing religiously. "That is, *the knowledge of God is given more in the presuppositions (the faith) with which experience is apprehended and interpreted than with the particularities or details of experience itself.*"[41] Or as Vincent Brümmer puts it: "the existence of Jahweh differs from the existence of things around us firstly in being necessary within the context of our faith."[42] So if faith-claims about God function as necessary statements within a religious form of life, then what needs to be explained is not God but the experiences we call evil. God is necessary, while the putative evils are contingent. In other words, while God cannot be other than he is, evil could be otherwise, i.e., good. However, the problem of evil is not merely due to contingency but to "the appearance" of intractability. This "appearance" seems to arise from a fear which is the expectation of evil rather than a fear which is the challenge to faith.

Thus, a phenomenological study of evil from the perspective of fear attends to the primary contexts from which meaning arises whether they be natural or supernatural. When all is suspended, in either context, we arrive at a consciousness poised for meaning through hopes and fears: these are the basic options of intentionality. And although one might successfully develop separate hermeneutics from these options, neither would be able to account for the perplexing ambiguities which "evil" mirrors. Rather, it is the dialectical synthesis of both which offers a propaedeutic to the problem. Such a synthesis constitutes a hermeneutic of fear and faith, as well as a reduction of experience to meaning and meaning to experience.

In the final analysis, the primacy of fear can be demonstrated in both the reductive and the productive processes of consciousness. Fear occasions a new interpretation of experience, one which either reaches below in despair or above in hope. However, within the religious context, fear synthesizes despair (the feeling of helplessness), and hope (the feeling of trust) to produce faith. Thus, faith becomes the inverse of fear, a transformation which leads to religious understanding. Nevertheless, both together constitute the experience of consciousness; that is, the meaning of experience and the experience of meaning.

NOTES

1. Wittgenstein, *Philosophical Investigations*, sec. 19.

2. Harold S. Kushner, *When Bad Things Happen to Good People* (New York: Avon Books, 1983), p. 75.

3. John Macquarrie, *God-Talk: An Examination of the Language and Logic of Theology* (New York: The Seabury Press, 1979), pp. 80-81.

4. Our "many approaches" to the understanding of disquietude underscore the point, variously made in the preceding chapters, that there are many ways of having objects. Equally important is the awareness that all our disquieting experiences have "objective" realities. Thus, the putative problem of evil—understood as the threat of non-being—is not without its "objective correlates." There is much warrant then to speak of fear and evil rather than *anxiety* and evil.

5. Genesis 3:6-7 (RSV).

6. It would appear that self-consciousness is always attracted to a comphrensive view of reality; at least, one that it wills. And as Hegel makes known, this comprehensive view is attempted via a dialectical process of separation, conflict, and meditation.

7. Genesis 3:10 (The New International Bibile).

8.   Rudolf Otto, *The Idea of the Holy*, trans. John W. Harvey (New York: Oxford University Press, 1958), p. 26.

9.   Genesis 3:17-19 (RSV).

10. Once a phenomenon is adjudged to be evil then it is the task of morality to elaborate on it. That is, to develop the principles which govern our relationship with it. So whereas fear is the medium through which evil is experienced, guilt is one of the ways of responding to personal acts which are considered evil. The one is a function of intentional consciousness, while the other is a function of conscience. But without fear guilt is powerless, if not non-existent. Thus fear enters our experience as a necessary step in the attribution, determination, and correction of evil.

11. James Plastaras, *Creation and Covenant* (Milwaukee: The Bruce Publishing Company, 1968), p. 55.

12. Ibid., p. 56.

13. Ibid., p. 55.

14. Don Ihde, *Hermeneutic Phenomenology: The Philosophy of Paul Ricoeur* (Evanston: Northwestern University Press, 1971), p. 29.

15. Macquarrie, *God-Talk...*, p. 80.

16. Ibid., p. 19.

17. Alan Keightley, *Wittgenstein, Grammar and God* (London: Epworth Press, 1976), p. 55.

18. Macquarrie, *God-Talk...*, p. 80, 99.

19. Paraphrase of Exodus 20:5.

20. Paul Ricoeur, "The Critique of Religion" and "The Language of Faith," trans. R. Bradley De Ford, *Union Seminary Quarterly Review* 28 (1973): 205-12; 213-24, quoted in Charles E. Reagan and David Stewart, ed., *The Philosophy of Paul Ricoeur* (Boston: Beacon Press, 1978), pp. 214-15; 234.

21. Psalm 14:1, 53:1. Proverbs goes on to say that "Wisdom is too high for a fool" (Proverbs 24:7); but the New Testament speaks of those who become fools in the eyes of the world so that they might fulfill the wisdom of Christ (I Corinthians 3:18).

22. Frederick Ferré, *Language, Logic and God* (New York: Harper Row Publishers, 1969), pp. 33, 25.

23. C. G. Jung, *Answer to Job*, trans. R. F. C. Hall (Princeton: Princeton University Press, 1973), p. xii.

24. Ibid., p. xi.

25.   John Wisdom, "Gods," in *Essays in Logic and Language*, ed. Antony Flew, First series (Oxford: Basil Blackwell, 1951), p. 197, quoted in Ferré, p. 133.

26.   Frederick Ferré, pp. 136-45.

27.   Some may even argue that evil is simply nature's peculiar way of discriminating against the weak (through natural selection, as it were), or that evil is nature's tendency toward (self-) destruction. But be that as it may, evil poses a formidable challenge to the optimism of reason and faith because it suggests that nature and experience are incomplete, and that completion is more a matter of hope than of fact.

28.   Gordon Kaufman, *God the Problem*, p. 199.

29.   Ibid., p. 98.

30.   Ibid., pp. 100, 89.

31.   Ibid., p. 106.

32.   John Hick, "Faith." in *The Encyclopedia of Philosophy*, ed. Paul Edwards (New York: Macmillan Publishing Company and the Free Press, 1967), vol. 3, p. 168.

33.   John Hick's assessment of Ireneanian theodicy as developmental underscores this point. William H. Willimon notes that:

"Irenaeus' idea that evil is justified only when we are able to stand in the future and look back on how well things have worked out has its counterpart in the developmental, evolutionary thought of later thinkers such as Hegel, Schleiermacher, and more recently, John Hick" (William H. Willimon, *Sighing for Eden: Sin, Evil and the Christian Faith* [Nashville: Abingdon Press, 1985], p. 55).

34. Charles Courtney, "Introduction" *The Problem of God in Philosophy of Religion*, by Henry Duméry, trans. Charles Courtney (Evanston: Northwestern University Press, 1964), p. xxx.

35. Frederick Sontag, "Anthropodicy and the Return of God," in *Encountering Evil: Live Options in Theodicy*, ed. Stephen T. David, Frederick Sontag, et al. (Atlanta: John Knox Press, 1981), p. 138.

36. Frederick Sontag, "Life and Death," *American Journal of Theology and Philosophy* 4 (May 1983): 63.

37. Gilbert Ryle, *The Concept of Mind* (New York: Barnes & Noble, 1949; reprinted edition, 1970).

38. *The Problem of God in Philosophy of Religion*, pp. cccviii-xxxix.

39. Ibid., p. 64, n. 24.

40. "Gott kannst du nicht mit einem Andern reden hören, sondern nur, wenn du der Angeredete bist.—Das ist eine grammatische Bemerkung." (Ludwig Wittgenstein, *Zettel*, ed. G. E. M. Ascombe and G. H. von Wright, trans. G. E. M. Ascombe [Berkeley, Los Angeles: University of California Press, 1970], p. 124).

41. Gordon Kaufman, *God the Problem*, p. 239.

42. Vincent Brümmer, *Theology and Philosophical Inquiry* (Philadelphia: The Westminster Press, 1982), pp. 286-87.

BIBLIOGRAPHY

Books

Works on Fear and Evil

Adams, Marilyn McCord and Robert Merrihew, eds. *The Problem of Evil*. Oxford: Oxford University Press, 1990.

Aquinas, Thomas. *Summa Contra Gentiles*. Translated by the English Dominican Fathers. London: Burns, Oates & Washburn, 1923.

_____ *Summa Theologiae*, vols. 1 and 2. Edited by Thomas Gilby. Garden City, New York: Image Books--A Division of Doubleday & Company, 1969.

Auden, W. H. *The Age of Anxiety*. New York: Random House, 1947.

Becker, Ernest. *The Denial of Death*. New York: The Free Press, 1973.

_____ *Escape From Evil*. New York: The Free Press, 1975.

_____ *The Structure of Evil*. New York: The Free Press, 1968.

Buber, Martin. *Good and Evil*. Translated by Michael Bullock. New York: Scribner & Sons, 1953.

Camus, Albert. *The Plague*. New York: Knopf, 1957.

Davis, Stephen T., Sontag, Frederick, et al. *Encountering Evil: Live Options in Theodicy*. Atlanta: John Knox Press, 1981.

Farrer, Austin. *Love Almighty and Ills Unlimited*. London: Collins/Fontana Press, 1962.

Ferré, Frederick. *Language, Logic and God*. New York: Harper & Row, Publishers, 1969.

Fiddes, Paul S. *The Creative Suffering of God*. Oxford: Claredon Press, 1992.

Fitch, William. *God and Evil*. London: Pickering & Inglis, 1967.

Flew, Antony, and MacIntyre, A., eds., *New Essays in Philosophical Theology*. London: SCM Press, 1955.

Freud, Sigmund. *The Future of An Illusion*. Revised and edited by James Strachey. Translated by W. D. Robson-Scott. Garden City, New York: Anchor Books--Doubleday & Company, 1964.

_____ *The Problem of Anxiety*. Translated by Henry A. Bunker. New York: W. W. Norton & Company, 1936.

Hick, John. *Evil and the God of Love*. Rev. ed. San Francisco: Harper & Row, Publishers, 1978.

Hiltner, Seward, and Menninger, Karl, ed. *Constructive Aspects of Anxiety*. New York: Abingdon Press, 1963.

Hume, David. *Dialogues Concerning Natural Religion.* Edited with an Introduction by Norman Kemp Smith. Indianapolis: Bobs-Merrill Press, 1980.

Journet, Charles. *The Meaning of Evil.* Translated by Michael Barry. New York: P. J. Kenedy, 1963.

Jung, Carl. *Answer to Job.* Translated by R. F. C. Hull. Princeton: Princeton University Press, 1973.

Kaufman, Gordon D. *God and Problem.* Cambridge, Mass.: Harvard University Press, 1972.

Kierkegaard, Sören. *The Concept of Dread.* Translated with an Introduction and Notes by Walter Lowrie. Princeton: Princeton University Press, 1957.

_____ *Fear and Trembling and Sickness Unto Death.* Translated with an Introduction and Notes by Walter Lowrie. Garden City, New York: Doubleday & Company, 1954.

Kushner, Harold S. *When Bad Things Happen to Good People.* New York: Avon Books, 1983.

Lewis, C. S. *The Problem of Pain.* New York: Macmillan Company, 1970 (10th printing).

Liebniz, G. W. *Theodicy.* Edited with an Introduction by Austin Farrer. Translated by E. M. Huggard. London: Routledge & Kegan Paul, 1952.

Lindström, Fredrik. *God and the Origin of Evil.* Liberforlag Lund, Sweden: CWK Gleerup, 1983.

Madden, Edward H., and Hare, Peter H. *Evil and the Concept of God.* American Lecture Series Publication, no. 706. Springfield, Illinois, 1968.

May, Rollo. *The Meaning of Anxiety.* New York: Ronald Press, Company, 1950.

Niebuhr, Reinhold. *The Nature and Destiny of Man*, vol. 1. New York: Scribner's Sons, 1941.

Nietzsche, Friedrich. *Beyond Good and Evil.* Translated with an Introduction and Commentary by R. J. Hollingdale. New York: Penguin Books, 1979.

_____ *The Birth of Tragedy.* Translated by Thomas Common. New York: Russell and Russell, 1964.

_____ *Thus Spoke Zarathustra.* Translated by Thomas Common. New York: Russell and Russell, 1964.

Noddings, Nel. *Women and Evil.* University of California Press, 1989.

Overstreet, Bonaro W. *Understanding Fear in Ourselves and Others.* New York: Harper & Brothers, Publishers, 1951.

Pfister, Oscar. *Christianity and Fear.* New York: Macmillan

Company, 1948.

Pike, Nelson, ed. *God and Evil: Readings on the Theological Problem of Evil.* Englewood Cliffs, N. J.: Prentice-Hall, 1964.

Plantinga, Alvin. *God, Freedom and Evil.* Grand Rapids, Michigan: William B. Eerdmans Publishing Company,1977.

_____ *Learning to Live with Evil.* Grand Rapids, Michigan: William B. Eerdmans Publishing Company, 1982.

Rice, P. B. *On the Knowledge of Good and Evil.* Westport, Connecticut: Greenwood Press, 1975.

Ricoeur, Paul. *The Symbolism of Evil.* Translated by E. Buchanan. New York: Harper & Row, 1967.

Rosenthal, Abigail L. *A Good Look at Evil.* Philadelphia: Temple University Press, 1987.

Rubenstein, Richard. *After Auschwitz.* New York: The Bobbs-Merrill Company, 1966.

Sluckin, Wladyslaw, ed. *Fear in Animals and Man.* New York: Van Nostrand Reinhold Company, 1979.

Sontag, Frederick. *The God of Evil.* New York: Harper & Row, 1970.

_____ *God, Why Did You Do That?* Philadelphia: Westminster Press, 1970.

Steinbeck, John. *The Grapes of Wrath.* New York: The Viking Press, 1939.

Sullivan, Harry S. *The Meaning of Anxiety in Psychiatry and in Life.* New York: The William Alanson White Institute, 1948.

Taylor, Richard. *Good and Evil: A New Direction.* New York: Prometheus Books, 1984.

Tillich, Paul. *The Courage to Be.* New Haven: Yale University Press, 1952.

Townes, Emilie M., ed. *A Troubling in My Soul: Womanist Perspectives On Evil & Suffering.* New York: Orbis Books, 1993.

Trau, Jane Mary. *The Co-Existence of God and Evil.* New York: Peter Lang, 1991.

Unamuno, Miguel de. *The Agony of Christianity.* Translated with an Introduction by Kurt F. Reinhardt. New York: Frederick Ungar Publishing Co., 1960.

_____ *Tragic Sense of Life.* Translated by J. E. Crawford Flitch. New York: Dover Publications, 1954.

Voltaire, F. M. A. *Candide*. Introduction by Philip Littell. New York: Modern Library, 1946.

Willimon, William H. *Sighing for Eden: Sin, Evil and the Christian Faith*. Nashville: Abingdon Press, 1985.

Supporting Themes

Allport, Gordon W. *The Individual and His Religion*. New York: The Macmillan Company, 1970.

Becker, Ernest. *Beyond Alienation*. New York: George Braziller, 1967.

Bierstedt, Robert. *Power and Progress*. New York: McGraw-Hill, 1974.

Brown, Norman O. *Life Against Death: The Psychoanalytic Meaning of History*. New York: Viking Press, 1959.

Brown, Seyom. *The Crisis of Power*. New York: Columbia University Press, 1968.

Carse, James P. *Death and Existence*. New York: John Wiley & Sons, 1980.

Choron, Jacques. *Death and Modern Man*. New York: Collier Books, 1964.

Feifel, Herman, ed. *The Meaning of Death*. New York: Collier-

Macmillan, 1972.

Flew, Anthony, ed. *Body, Mind, and Death*. New York: Macmillan Co., 1971.

Friedrich, Carl J., and Blitzer, Charles. *The Age of Power*. New York: Cornell University Press, 1967.

Fromm, Erich. *The Anatomy of Human Destructiveness*. New York: Holt, Rinehart and Winston, 1973.

Hobbes, Thomas. *Leviathan*. Oxford: The Clarendon Press, 1909 (reprinted from the 1651 edition).

Israel, Joachim. *Alienation: From Marx to Modern Sociology*. Boston: Allyn and Bacon, 1971.

Jung, Carl. *Modern Man in Search of a Soul*. Translated by W. S. Dell and Cary F. Baynes. New York: Harcourt, Brace and World, 1966.

_____ *Psychology of the Unconscious*. Translated by Beatrice Hinkle. New York: Dodd, Mead, 1957.

Kaplan, Morton A. *Alienation and Identification*. New York: The Free Press, 1976.

Krieger, Leonard and Stern, Fritz, ed. *The Responsibility of Power: Historical Essays in Honor of Hajo Holborn*. Garden City, New York: Doubleday & Company, 1976.

Kübler-Ross, Elisabeth. *On Death and Dying*. New York: Macmillan Company, 1969.

Laski, Harold J. *A Grammar of Politics*. 2nd ed. New Haven: Yale University Press, 1931.

Laswell, Harold, and Harlan, Cleveland, ed. *The Ethics of Power: The Interplay of Religion, Philosophy and Politics*. New York: Harper & Brothers, 1976.

Laswell, Harold Dwight. *Power and Personality*. New York: W. W. Norton and Company, 1976.

Laswell, Harold Dwight, and Kaplan Abraham. *Power and Society: A Framework for Political Inquiry*. The Hague: Martinus Nijhoff, 1966.

Lee, Dorothy. *Freedom and Culture*. Englewood Cliffs, N. J.: Prentice-Hall, 1959.

Machiavelli, Niccolo. *The Prince*. Translated from Italian by Ninain H. Thompson. 2nd ed., rev. and corrected. Oxford: The Clarendon Press, 1897.

May, Rollo. *Power and Innocence*. New York: Dell Publishing Company, 1972.

Messarman, Jules, ed. *The Dynamics of Power*. New York: Grane and Stratton, 1972.

Mueller-Deham, Albert. *Human Relations and Power*. New York: Philosophical Library, 1957.

Nietzsche, Friedrich. *The Will to Power*. Translated by Thomas Common. New York: Russel and Russel, 1964.

Oglesby, Carl, and Shaull, Richard. *Containment and Change*. New York: Macmillan Company, 1967.

Pringle-Pattison. A. Seth. *The Idea of Immortality*. Gifford Lecture. Oxford: The Clarendon Press, 1922.

Rank, Otto. *The Trauma of Birth*. New York: Harcourt, Brace & Co., 1929.

_____ *Will, Therapy, and Truth and Reality*. New York: Knopf Publishers, 1936.

Russell, Bertrand. *Power*. New York: W. W. Norton & Company, 1969.

Schacht, Richard. *Alienation*. Introduction by Walter Kaufmann. London: Allen & Unwin, 1971.

Schwartz, David C. *Political Alienation and Political Behavior*. Chicago: Aldine Publishing Company, 1973.

Stein, M. R.; Vidich, A. J.; and White, D., ed. *Identity and Anxiety: Survival of the Person in Mass Society*. New York: The Free Press, 1960.

Sykes, Gerald, ed. *Alienation: The Cultural Climate of Our Time.* New York: George Braziller, 1964.

Tillich, Paul. *Love, Power and Justice: Ontological Analyses and Ethical Applications.* New York: Oxford University Press, 1954.

Toynbee, Arnold, ed. *Man's Concern with Death.* London: Hodder & Stoughton, 1968.

Weisskopf, Walter A. *Alienation and Economics.* New York: Dutton, 1971.

Methodological Sources

Chapman, Harmon M. *Sensations and Phenomenology.* Bloomington: The University of Indiana Press, 1966.

Chisholm, Roderick, ed. *Realism and the Background of Phenomenology.* Glencoe, Illinois: The Free Press, 1961.

Derrida, Jacques. *Speech and Phenomena and Other Essays on Husserl's Theory of Signs.* Translated with an Introduction by David B. Allison. Evanston: Northwestern University Press, 1973.

Edie, James M. *Speaking and Meaning: The Phenomenology of Language.* Bloomington: The Indiana University Press, 1973.

Embree, Lester E., ed. *Life-world and Consciousness: Essays for Aron Gurwitsch.* Evanston: Northwestern University Press, 1972.

Farber, Marvin. *The Aims of Phenomenology.* New York: Harper & Row, Publishers, 1966.

_____ *The Foundation of Phenomenology.* 2nd. ed. New York: Paine-Whitman, 1962.

Gier, Nicholas. *Wittgenstein and Phenomenology.* Albany: The State University of New York Press. 1981.

Greenspan, Patricia S. *Emotions and Reasons: An Inquiry into Emotional Justification.* New York/London: Routledge,1988.

Gurwitsch, Aron. *The Field of Consciousness.* Evanston: Northwestern University Press, 1964.

Husserl, Edmund. *The Crisis of European Sciences and Transcendental Phenomenology.* Translated by David Carr. Evanston: Northwestern University Press, 1970.

_____ *Experience and Judgment: Investigations in a Genealogy of Logic.* Revised and edited by Ludwig Langrebe. Translated by James Churchill and Karl Ameriks. Evanston: Northwestern University Press, 1973.

_____ *Formal and Transcendental Logic.* Translated by Dorian

Cairns. The Hague: Martinus Nijhoff, 1969.

Husserl, Edmund. *Ideas: General Introduction to Pure Phenomenology.* Translated by W. R. Boyce-Gibson. London: Collier Books, Collier-Macmillan, 1969.

____ *The Logical Investigations.* Translated by J. N. Findlay. London: Routledge & Kegan Paul, 1970. Vols. 1 and 2.

Ihde, Don. *Hermeneutic Phenomenology: The Philosophy of Paul Ricoeur.* Evanston: Northwestern University Press, 1971.

____ *Sense and Significance.* Pittsburgh: Duquesne University Press, 1973.

Kohák, Erazim. *Idea and Experience: Edmund Husserl's Project of Phenomenology in Ideas 1.* Chicago: The University of Chicago Press, 1978.

Laszlo, Ervin. *Beyond Scepticism and Realism: A Constructive Exploration of Husserlian and Whiteheadian Methods of Inquiry.* The Hague: Martinus Nijhoff, 1966.

McAllister, Linda, ed. *The Philosophy of Brentano.* London: Geral Duckworth & Company, 1976.

Malcolm, Norman. *Wittgenstein...A Religious Point of View?* (edited with a response by Peter Winch). New York:Cornell University Press, 1994.

Mall, Ram Adhar. *Experience and Reason: The Phenomenology of Edmund Husserl and Its Relation to Hume's Philosophy.* The Hague: Martinus Nijhoff, 1937.

Mensch, James R. *The Question of Being in Husserl's Investigations.* The Hague: Martinus Nijhoff, 1981.

Merleau-Ponty, Maurice. *Consciousness and the Acquisition of Language.* Evanston: Northwestern University Press, 1973.

_____ *The Structure of Behavior.* Boston: Beacon Press, 1963.

Mohanty, J. N. *Edmund Husserl's Theory of Meaning.* The Hague: Martinus Nijhoff, 1964.

Monk, Ray. *Ludwig Wittgenstein: The Duty of Genius.* New York, Penguin Books, 1991.

Philan, G. B. *Feeling Experience and Its Modalities.* London: Routledge and Kegan Paul, 1925.

Ricoeur, Paul. *Freud and Philosophy: An Essay on Interpretation.* New Haven: Yale University Press, 1970.

_____ *Husserl: An Analysis of His Phenomenology.* Evanston: Northwestern University Press, 1967.

_____ *Interpretation Theory: Discourse and the Surplus of Meaning.* Fort Worth, Texas: Texas University Press,

1976.

Sokolowski, Robert. *The Formation of Husserl's Concept of Constitution*. The Hague: Martinus Nijhoff, 1964.

_____ *Presence and Absence: A Philosophical Investigation of Language and Being*. Bloomington: The University of Indiana Press, 1974.

Solomon, Robert C. *The Passions: The Myth and Nature of Human Emotion*. Indiana: The University of Notre Dame Press, 1983.

Spiegelberg, Herbert. *The Context of the Phenomenological Movement*. The Hague: Martinus Nijhoff, 1981.

_____ *Doing Phenomenology*. The Hague: Martinus Nijhoff, 1975.

_____ *The Phenomenological Movement*, vols. 1 and 2. The Hague: Martinus Nijhoff, 1960.

Stevens, R. *James and Husserl: The Foundations of Meaning*. The Hague: Martinus Nijhoff, 1974.

Strasser, Stephan. *Phenomenology and the Human Sciences*. Duquesne Studies, Psychological Series #1. Pittsburgh: Duquesne University Press, 1963.

_____ *The Phenomenology of Feeling*. Translated with an

Introduction by Robert E. Wood. Foreword by Paul Ricoeur. Pittsburgh: Duquesne University Press, 1977.

Straus, E. *The Primary World of the Senses: A Vindication of Sensory Experience.* Translated by J. Needleman. New York: The Free Press, 1963.

Welton, Donn. *The Origins of Meaning: A Critical Study of the Thresholds of Husserlian Phenomenology.* The Hague: Martinus Nijhoff, 1983.

Wittgenstein, Ludwig. *Last Writings in the Philosophy of Psychology.* Edited by G. H. von Wright and Heikki Nyman. Translated by C. G. Luckhardt and A. E. Maximillan. Chicago: The University of Chicago Press, 1982.

_____ *Lectures and Conversations in Aesthetics, Psychology and Religious Belief.* Edited by Cyril Barrett. Berkeley: The University of California Press, 1966.

_____ *Philosophical Grammar.* Edited by Anthony Kenny. Translated by Rush Rhees. Berkeley: The University of California Press, 1974.

_____ *Philosophical Investigations.* Translated by G. E. M. Anscombe. Oxford: Basil Blackwell, 1958.

_____ *Tractatus Logico-Philosophicus.* London: Routledge & Kegan Paul, reprint ed., 1971.

_____ *Zettel*. Edited by G. E. M. Anscombe and G. H. von Wright. Translated by G. E. M. Anscombe. Berkeley: The University of California Press, 1970.

Supplementary Sources

Arendt, Hannah. *The Human Condition*. Chicago: The University of Chicago Press, 1958.

Austin, J. L. *How To Do Things With Words*. Cambridge, Mass.: Harvard University Press, 1962.

_____ *Sense and Sensibilia*. Oxford: The Clarendon Press, 1962.

Ayer, A. J., ed. *Logical Positivism*. Glencoe, Illinois: The Free Press, 1959.

Baelz, Peter R. *Christian Theology and Metaphysics*. Philadelphia: Fortress Press, 1968.

Becker, Ernest. *The Revolution in Psychiatry*. New York: The Free Press, 1964.

Brown, Stuart C. *Do Religious Claims Make Sense?* London: SCM Press, 1969.

Brümmer, Vincent. *Theology and Philosophical Inquiry* Philadelphia: The Westminster Press, 1982.

Cavell, Stanley. *Must We Mean What We Say?* Cambridge, England: Cambridge University Press, 1976.

Chomsky, Noam. *Language and Mind.* New York: Harcourt, Brace, Jovanovich, 1972.

_____ *Reflections on Language.* New York: Random House, 1975.

_____ *Syntactic Structures.* The Hague: Mouton, 1957.

Church, Joseph. *Language and the Discovery of Reality.* New York: Random House, 1961.

Cohen, Jonathan. *The Diversity of Meaning.* New York: Herder and Herder, 1963.

Darwin, Charles. *The Expression of the Emotions in Man and Animals.* London: London University Press, 1872; re-edited by the University of Chicago Press, 1965.

Descartes, René. *Philosophical Writings--A Selection.* Translated and edited by Elizabeth Anscombe and Peter Geach. Edinburgh: The Nelson Philosophical Texts, 1959.

Dilley, Frank B. *Metaphysics and Religious Language.* New York: Columbia University Press, 1964.

Duméry, Henry. *The Problem of God in Philosophy of Religion.* Translated with an Introduction by Charles Courtney.

Evanston: Northwestern University Press, 1964.

Flew, Anthony, ed. *Essays in Logic and Language*. First series. Oxford: Basil Blackwell, 1951.

Fodor, J. A., and Katz, J. J., ed. *The Structure of Language*. Englewood Cliffs, N. J.: Prentice-Hall, 1964.

Gadamer, Hans-Georg. *Philosophical Hermeneutics*. Translated and edited by David E. Linge. Berkeley: The University of California Press, 1976.

_____ *Truth and Method*. Translated by Garrett Barden and John Cumming. New York: The Crossroad Publishing Company, 1984.

Gustafson, Donald F., ed. *Essays in Philosophical Psychology*. New York: Anchor Books, Doubleday Company, 1964.

Hampshire, Stuart. *Thought and Action*. London: Chatto and Windus, 1960.

Hegel, G. F. W. *Early Theological Writings*. 4th ed. Translated by T. M. Knox. Introduction by Richard Kroner. Philadelphia: University of Pennsylvania Press, 1981.

_____ *Phenomenology of Spirit*. Translated with an analysis of the text by A. V. Miller. Foreword by J. N. Findlay. Oxford: Oxford University Press, 1981.

Heidegger, Martin. *Being and Time*. Translated by John Macquarrie and Edward Robinson. New York: Harper & Row, Publishers, 1962.

_____ *Hegel's Concept of Experience*. Translated by J. Glenn Gray and Fred Wieck. New York: Harper & Row, Publishers, 1970.

_____ *On the Way to Language*. Translated by Peter D. Hertz and Joan Stambaugh. New York: Harper & Row, Publishers, 1972.

Hendry, George. *The Theology of Nature*. Philadelphia: The Westminster Press, 1980.

High, Dallas. *Language, Persons, and Belief*. New York: Oxford University Press, 1967.

James, William. *Essays in Radical Empiricism*. London: Longmans, Green, 1912.

_____ *Principles of Psychology*. New York: Hold, 1890.

_____ *The Varieties of Religious Experience*. Introduction by Reinhold Niebuhr. London: Collier-Macmillan, Publishers, 1979.

Kant, Immanuel. *Critique of Judgement*. Translated with an Introduction by J. H. Bernard. New York: Hafner Publishing Co., 1951.

_____ *Critique of Pure Reason.* Translated by Norman Kemp Smith. London: Macmillan Co., 1958.

Keightley, Alan. *Wittgenstein, Grammar and God.* London: Epworth Press, 1976.

Kenny, Anthony. *Action, Emotion and Will.* London: Routledge & Kegan Paul, 1963.

Langer, Suzanne K. *Feeling and Form.* New York: Penguin Books, 1953.

Lawrence, Irene. *Linguistics and Theology: The Significance of Noam Chomsky for Theological Construction.* Metuchen, N. J.: The Scarecrow Press, 1980.

Lemos, Ramon M. *Experience Mind and Value.* Leiden: E. J. Britt, 1969.

Lewis, C. I. *Mind and the World Order.* New York: Dover Press, 1956.

Macquarrie, John. *God-Talk: An Examination of the Language and Logic of Theology.* New York: The Seabury Press, 1979.

Norris, Charles. *Signs, Language and Behavior.* New York: Braziller, 1946.

Muzorewa, Gwinyai H. *The Origins and Development of African*

Theology. Maryknoll, New York: Orbis Books, 1985.

Nozick, Robert. *Philosophical Explanations*. Cambridge, Mass.: The Belknap Press of Harvard University, 1981.

Oakeshott, Michael. *Experience and Its Modes*. Cambridge, England: Cambridge University Press, 1933.

Ogden, C. K., and Richards, I. A. *The Meaning of Meaning*. New York: Harcourt, Brace, 1923.

Otto, Rudolf. *The Idea of the Holy*. Translated by John W. Harvey. New York: Oxford University Press, 1958.

Palmer, Richard E. *Hermeneutics: Interpretation Theory in Schleiermacher, Dilthey, Heidegger, and Gadamer*. Evanston: Northwestern University Press, 1969.

Phillips, D. Z., ed. *Religion and Understanding*. Oxford: Basil Blackwell, 1967.

Plastaras, James. *Creation and Covenant*. Milwaukee: The Bruce Publishing Company, 1968.

Ramsay, Ian T. *Religious Language: An Empirical Placing of Theological Phrases*. London: SCM Press, 1957.

Reagan, Charles E., and Steward, David, eds. *The Philosophy of Paul Ricoeur*. Boston: Beacon Press, 1978.

Richardson, John T. E. *The Grammar of Justification: An Interpretation of Wittgenstein's Philosophy of Language.* New York: St. Martin's Press, 1976.

Rorty, Richard, ed. *The Linguistic Turn: Recent Essays in Philosophical Method.* Chicago: The University of Chicago Press, 1968.

Russell, Bertrand. *The Problems of Philosophy.* New York: H. Holt & Company, 1912.

Ryle, Gilbert. *The Concept of Mind.* New York: Barnes and Noble, 1965.

Sartre, Jean-Paul. *Being and Nothingness.* Translated by Hazel Barnes. New York: The Philosophical Library, 1956.

_____ *The Emotions: Outline of a Theory.* New York: The Philosophical Library, 1948.

Schleiermacher, F. D. E. *Hermeneutics: The Handwritten Manuscripts.* Edited by H. Kimmerle. Translated by J. Duke and J. Fortsman. Missoula, Montana: Scholars Press, 1977.

Schopenhauer, Arthur. *The World as Will and Idea.* Translated by R. B. Haldane and I. Kemp (9th imprint). 3 vols. London: Routledge & Kegan Paul, 1948.

Searle, John. *Speech Acts: An Essay in the Philosophy of*

Language. London: Cambridge University Press, 1969.

Sefler, George F. *Language and World: A Methodological Synthesis Within the Writings of Martin Heidegger and Ludwig Wittgenstein*. Englewood Cliffs, N. J.: Humanities Press, 1974.

Sokolowski, Robert. *Presence and Absence: A Philosophical Investigation of Language and Being*. Bloomington: The University of Indiana Press, 1974.

Solomon, Robert C. *From Rationalism to Existentialism: The Existentialists and Their Nineteenth-Century Background*. New York: Humanities Press, 1970.

Spanos, William V. *A Casebook on Existentialism*. New York: Thomas Y. Crowell Company, 1966.

Strawson, P. F. *Individuals: An Essay in Descriptive Methphysics*. London: Methuen, 1959.

Taylor, A. E. *Plato: The Man and His Work*. New York: The Dial Press, 1936.

Taylor, Charles. *Hegel*. Cambridge: Cambridge University Press, 1975.

Thiselton, Anthony. *The Two Horizons: New Testament Hermeneutics and Philosophical Description*. Grand Rapids, Michigan: William B. Eerdman's Publishing Co.,

1980.

Urban, W. N. *Language and Reality*. London: Allen & Unwin, 1961.

Wheelwright, Philip. *Metaphor and Reality*. Bloomington: Indiana University Press, 1962.

Articles

Adams, Marilyn McCord. "Problems of Evil: More Advice to Christian Philosophies" *Faith and Philosophy*, Vol. 5, No. 2 (April 1988): 121-143.

Bar-Hillel, Y. "Husserl's Conception of a Purely Logical Grammar." *Philosophy and Phenomenological Research* 17 (1967).

Burrell, J. J., and Burrell, J. E. "A Self-directed Approach for a Science of Human Experience." *Journal of Phenomenological Psychology*, no. 6 (1975): 63-75.

Buytendijk, F. J. J. "The Phenomenological Approach to the Problem of Feelings and Emotions." In *Feelings and Emotions*. Edited by M. L. Reymert. New York: McGraw-Hill, 1950.

Cairns, Dorian. "The Ideality of Verbal Expressions." *Philosophy and Phenomenological Research* 1 (1940): 98-109.

Chadwick, Mary. "Notes Upon the Fear of Death." *International Journal of Psychoanalysis* 10 (1929).

Chomsky, Noam. "Deep Structure, Surface Structure, and Semantic Interpretation." In *Semantics*. Edited by D. D. Steinberg and L. A. Jakobovits. London: Cambridge University Press, 1969.

Compton, John J. "Hare, Husserl, and Philosophic Discovery." *Dialogue* 111 (1964): 42-51.

Crosson, F. J. "The Concept of Mind and the Concept of Consciousness." In *Phenomenology in America*. Edited by James M. Edie. Chicago: Quadrangle Books, 1967.

Dupre, Louis "Evil: A Religious Mastery" *Faith and Philosophy* Vol. 7, No. 3 (July 1990): 261-280.

Edie, James M. "Can Grammar Be Thought." In *Patterns of the Life-World*. Edited by James M. Edie, F. H. Parker, and C. O. Schrag. Evanston: Northwestern University Press, 1970.

_____ "Necessary Truth and Perception: William James on the Structure of Experience." In *New Essays in Phenomenology*, pp. 254ff. Chicago: Quadrangle Books, 1969.

Feuer, Lewis. "What is Alienation? The Career of a Concept." *New Politics* 1 (Spring 1962): 116-34.

Firth, J. R. "Modes of Meaning." In *Essays and Studies*, pp. 118-49. London: English Association, 1951.

Fischer, W. F. "The Faces of Anxiety." *Journal of Phenomenological Psychology* 1 (1970): 31-49.

_____ "On the Phenomenological Mode of Researching 'Being Anxious.'" *Journal of Phenomenological Psychology* 4 (1974): 405-23.

Føllesdal, Dagfin. "Meaning and Experience." In *Mind and Language*. Edited by Samuel Guttenplan. Oxford: The Clarendon Press, 1975.

Garver, Newton. "Analyticity and Grammar." *The Monist* 51 (July 1967): 397-425.

Gelven, Michael. "The Meanings of evil." *Philosophy Today* 27 (Fall 1983): 200-21.

Gilbert, G. S., and Rappoport L. "Categories of Thought and Variations in Meaning." *Journal of Phenomenological Psychology* 5 (1975): 419-24.

Gill, Jerry H. "Wittgenstein and Religious Language." *Theology Today* 21 (1964): 59-72.

Goodman, Nelson. "On Likeness of Meaning." *Analysis* 10 (1949): 1-7.

Gordon, Robert M. "Fear." *The Philosophical Review* 89 (October 1980): 560-78.

Gurwitsch, Aron. "Edmund Husserl's Conception of Phenomenological Psychology." *Review of Metaphysics* 19 (June 1966): 689-727.

Haag, Herbert. "The Devil in Judaism and Christianity." *Theology Digest* 32 (Spring 1985): 29-32.

Haller, E. "On the Interpretive Task." *Interpretation* 21 (1967):158-67.

Halliday, M. A. K. "Categories of the Theory of Grammar." *Word* 17 (1961): 241-92.

Hallie, P. P. "Wittgenstein's Grammatical-Empirical Distinction." Journal of Philosophy 60 (1963): 565-78.

Harman, Gilbert H. "Three Levels of Meaning." *The Journal of Philosophy* 65 (October 3, 1968): 590-602.

Hasker, William "The Necessity of Gratuitous Evil" *Faith and Philosophy* Vol. 9, No. 1 (January 1992): 23-44.

Heath, P. L. "Experience." In *The Encyclopedia of Philosophy*, pp. 156-59. Edited by Paul Edwards. New York: The Macmillan Company & The Free Press, 1967.

Heilbrunn, Gert. "The Basic Fear." *Journal of the American*

Psychoanalytic Association 111 (1955): 447-66.

Hick, John. "Faith." In *The Encyclopedia of Philosophy*, vol. 3. Edited by Paul Edwards. New York: Macmillan Publishing Company & The Free Press, 1967.

Homans, Peter. "Psychology and Hermeneutics." *Journal of Religion* 60 (1975): 327-47.

Horowitz, Irving L. "On Alienation and the Social Order." *Philosophy and Phenomenological Research* 27 (December 1966): 230-37.

Katz, Jerrold J. "Mentalism in Linguistics." *Language* 40 (1964):124-37.

_____ "The Philosophical Relevance of Linguistic Theory." In *The Linguistic Turn*. Edited with an Introduction by Richard Rorty. Chicago: The University of Chicago Press, 1970.

Kaufman, Arnold S. "On Alienation." *Inquiry* 8 (Summer 1965):141-65.

Kavka, Gregory S. "Rule by Fear." *Nous* 17 (1983): 601-20.

Kimmerle, Heinz. "Hermeneutical Theory or Ontological Hermeneutics." *Journal for Theology and the Church* 4 (1967): 107-21.

Klein, Melanie. "The Theory of Anxiety and Guilt." In

210   *Bibliography*

Development of Psychoanalysis. Edited by Joan Riviere. London: Hogarth Press, 1952.

Kracklauer, C. "Exploring the Life-world." *Journal of Phenomenological Psychology* 2 (1972): 207-36.

Kuntz, Paul G. "Order in Language, Phenomena, and Realty: Notes on Linguistic Analysis, Phenomenology, and Metaphysics." *Monist* 49 (1965): 107-36.

Langer, Suzanne. "Origins of speech and it Communicative Function." *Quarterly Journal of Speech* (April 1960): 121-34.

Leifer, Ronald. "Avoidance and Mastery: An Interactional View of Phobias." *Journal of Individual Psychology* (May 1966): 80-93.

Levin, David Michael. "The Three Stages of Understanding: The Naive, the Scientific and the Phenomenological." In *Reason and Evidence in Husserl's Phenomenology*, pp. 3-32. Edited by David Michael Levin. Evanston: Northwestern University Press, 1970.

Levy, C. E. "Toward Primordial Reality as the Ground of Psychological Phenomena." *Journal of Phenomenological Psychology* (1973): 173-86.

Maritain, Jacque. "The Concept of Sovereignty." *American Political Science Review* 44 (1950).

McFarlane, Adrian A., Murrell, N. S. "Influences of the 19th Century Hermeneutics of Consciousness on Subsequent Modes of Understanding" *Correlatives*, Volume 2, Drew University, N. J. (Spring '88): 4-17.

Meissner, W. "The Implications of Experience for Psychological Theory." *Philosophy and Phenomenological Research,* no. 24 (1966): 503-28.

Merleau-Ponty, Maurice. "The Body as Expression and Speech." In *Phenomenology of Perception*, pp. 174-99. Translated by Colin Smith. London: Routledge & Kegan Paul, 1962.

_____ "The Phenomenology of Language." In *Signs*, pp. 84-97. By Maurice Merleau-Ponty. Translated by Richard McCleary. Evanston: Northwestern University Press, 1966.

Macquarrie, John. "Feeling and Understanding." In *Studies in Christian Existentialism*. By John Macquarrie. London: SCM Press, 1966.

Newsweek. "The Fight to Conquer Fear." April 23, 1984. *New York.* Weekly magazine. November 26, 1984.

Niebuhr, R. R. "Schleiermacher on Language and Feeling." *Theology Today* 17 (April 1960): 150-67.

Peacocke, Christopher. "Critical Study: Wittgenstein and Experience." *The Philosophical Quarterly* 32 (April 1982).

Quay, Paul M. "The Disvalue of Ontic Evil." *Theological Studies* 46 (1985): 262-86.

Ragan, R. S. "Cassirer and Wittgenstein." *International Philosophical Quarterly* 7 (1967).

Ranklin, K. W. "Wittenstein on Meaning, Understanding, and Intending." *American Philosophical Quarterly* 3 (January 1966): 1-13.

Ricoeur, Paul. "Husserl and Wittgenstein on Language." In *Phenomenology and Existentialism.* Edited by Edward N. Lee and Maurice Mandelbaum. Baltimore: The John Hopkins Press, 1967.

_____ "Schleiermacher's Hermeneutics." *Monist* 60 (April 1977): 181-97.

(von) Rintelen, F. J. "Philosophical Idealism in Germany: The Way from Kant to Hegel and the Present." *Philosophy and Phenomenological Research* 38 (September 1977): 1-32.

Roberts, Robert C. "Emotions As An Access To Religious Truths" *Faith and Philosophy*, Vol. 9, No. 1 (January 1992): 83-94.

Rorty, Amelie O. "Fearing Death." *Philosophy* 58 (April 1983). Russell, Bruce. "The Persistent Problem of Evil" *Faith and Philosophy*, Vol. 6, No. 2 (April 1989): 121-139.

Schachtel, Ernest G. "On Alienated Concept of Identity." *The American Journal of Psychoanalysis* 21 (1961): 120-30.

Schlesinger, G. "The Problem of Evil and the Problem of Suffering." *American Philosophical Quarterly* 1 (July 1964): 244-47.

Schur, Max. "The Ego in Anxiety." In *Drives, Affects, Behaviour*. Edited by Rudolph Loewenstein. New York: International Universities Press, 1953.

Solomon, Robert C. "Sense and Essence—Frege and Husserl." *International Philosophical Quarterly* 11 (1970).

Sontag, Frederick. "Life and Death." *American Journal of Theology* 4 (May 1983): 55-63.

Spiegelberg, Herbert. "Toward a Phenomenology of Experience." *American Philosophical Quarterly* 1 (October 1964).

Stambaugh, Joan. "The Greatest and Most Extreme Evil." *Philosophy Today* 27 (Fall 1983): 222-29.

Te Hennepe, E. "The Life-world and the World of Ordinary Language." In *An Invitation to Phenomenology*. Edited by James M. Edie. Chicago: Quadrangle Books, 1965.

Tranoy, K. E. "Contemporary Philosophy: The Analytic—The Continental." *Philosophy Today* 8 (1964).

Welton, Donn. "World and Consciousness." In *The Phenomenology of Edmund Husserl—Six Essays*, pp. 13-30. By Ludwig Langrebe. Edited with an Introduction by Donn Welton. Ithaca: Cornell University Press, 1981.

Yankelovich, Daniel. "Power and the Two Revolutions." In *The Dynamics of Power*. Edited by Jules H. Messerman. New York: Greene & Stratton, 1972.

Ziff, Paul. "About Ungrammaticalness." *Mind* 13 (1964): 204-14.

Studies in European Thought

This series of monographs, translations, and critical editions covers comparative and interdisciplinary topics of significance from the early eighteenth century to the present. Volumes, both published and projected, include a collection of essays on German drama, a study of the Künstlerroman, and a study on the aesthetics of the double talent of Kubin and Herzmanovsky-Orlando.